W0043180

WAFADARI
IMAANDARI
ZIMMEDARI

WAFADARI IMAANDARI ZIMMEDARI

War Room *to* Boardroom

LT GEN. K.J.S. 'TINY' DHILLON (RETD)

PENGUIN
VEER

An imprint of Penguin Random House

PENGUIN VEER

Penguin Veer is an imprint of the Penguin Random House group of companies whose addresses can be found at global.penguinrandomhouse.com

Published by Penguin Random House India Pvt. Ltd
4th Floor, Capital Tower 1, MG Road,
Gurugram 122 002, Haryana, India

First published in Penguin Veer by Penguin Random House India 2025

Copyright © Lt Gen. K.J.S. 'Tiny' Dhillon (Retd) 2025

All rights reserved

10 9 8 7 6 5 4

The views and opinions expressed in this book are the author's own and the facts are as reported by him which have been verified to the extent possible, and the publishers are not in any way liable for the same.

Please note that no part of this book may be used or reproduced in any manner for the purpose of training artificial intelligence technologies or systems.

ISBN 9780670098828

Typeset in EB Garamond by MAP Systems, Bengaluru, India
Printed at Thomson Press India Private Limited

This book is sold subject to the condition that it shall not, by way of trade or otherwise, be lent, resold, hired out or otherwise circulated without the publisher's prior consent in any form of binding or cover other than that in which it is published and without a similar condition including this condition being imposed on the subsequent purchaser.

www.penguin.co.in

*To Bolt, our most wafadar companion for almost
fourteen years*

Travel well, buddy!

God bless you!

BOLT
(29 January 2010–22 August 2023)

Contents

A Note of Love, Affection & Gratitude

Dear Readers,

Greetings! I hope you are doing well. My first book, *Kitne Ghazi Aaye, Kitne Ghazi Gaye* (*KGAKGG*), has been an immensely satisfying literary journey along with you over the last two years. Your love and affection for this soldier's debut book are overwhelming.

I would like to take a moment to express my deepest gratitude to all my readers for the support you've shown to *KGAKGG*. Your support made a difference and inspired me to pen down my four-decade leadership experiences with you in the form of *Wafadari, Imaandari, Zimmedari: War Room to Boardroom (WIZ)*.

Happy Reading
Read Good Books
Read Original Books
Thank you,

Jai Hind

Sincerely,
Lt Gen. K.J.S. '*Tiny*' Dhillon (Retd)

1

I See What Shines in You

'Leadership is a journey, not a destination. It is a marathon, not a sprint. It is a process, not an outcome.'
—John Donahoe, CEO, Nike

'**I see what shines in you**'—this simple but profound eulogy came my way from a charming lady I met for the first time in my life at a literary seminar in Chandigarh in February 2024. The occasion happened to coincide with the period when I was engaged in preparing the blueprint for my second book, which is this one. I had been invited to this 'Members only' literary event to participate in an interactive session to discuss my first book *Kitne Ghazi Aaye, Kitne Ghazi Gaye*. I was seated in the front row waiting for my session to begin when a graceful lady walked in and asked if she could sit in the vacant seat next to mine, after she had ostensibly failed to find any preferred seat in the rest of the hall. I politely gestured that she was welcome to sit there, and in accordance with the customary military civility that comes unbidden to a soldier due to the discipline imbibed after years of being in the army, I rose and wished her, 'Good morning, Ma'am', sitting down only after she had settled in her seat. After a while, as a precursor to my session, my photograph in full military uniform was displayed on the screen on stage along with a reading of my biodata. Surprised, the lady seated next to me turned and asked, 'Is that you?' I politely replied in the affirmative before moving up to the stage. After the session, some of the attendees complimented me for my services in the army, exchanging pleasantries and requests for some selfies.

I ran into this graceful lady again a few months later at another literary event that was attended by the same audience as the previous one. Instantly recognizing me, she recalled our encounter at the earlier event, which I, too, remembered vividly. She recounted that she had narrated that incident to her parents, too, telling them that she had instantly guessed my military antecedents from my gracious behaviour, which was confirmed when I was introduced and invited on stage by the master of ceremonies on that occasion. It is then that she delivered her potent one-liner that absolutely caught me unawares, '**I see what shines in you**—your gentlemanly mannerisms and upbringing are instantly visible to anyone you come across.' At that moment, I was too overwhelmed by the compliment to offer a suitable reaction, as I am sure anyone would have been. However, it was only later, as I ran through her words in my mind again, that I realized that the person who had stood up in deference to the lady in the hall was not me, K.J.S. Dhillon, but an officer of the Indian Army whose demeanour and actions had been conditioned by a strict military ethos and rigorous training, which has made such gentlemanly behaviour a way of life for all those who don the military uniform. So, yes, the inner 'shine' imparted to me by my four-decade long service in the army was obvious to any onlooker, especially a clairvoyant lady who could recognize the value of that chivalry.

What Is It That Shines in Me?

The entire process of chiselling, moulding, polishing and buffing of the rough edges of a teenager's personality to create the inner 'shine' began over forty-five years ago, on 2 January 1980. The chilly evening when I, as a strapping lad of seventeen years, boarded the popular Punjab Mail train from Ferozepur to reach the hallowed gates of the National Defence Academy (NDA) at Khadakwasla, is still fresh in my memory. Barely out of school, I plunged into the deep waters of army pedagogy, when, after a stringent selection procedure, I was called to join the NDA, widely known as the 'Cradle for Military Leadership'. The lanky boy, who had just started growing a wisp of a moustache, and who loved to sleep well past sunrise, was suddenly thrown into an alien world that was the complete antithesis of his hitherto easy-going life. However, it was the challenges of this highly regimented and disciplined environment at the NDA and subsequently at the Indian Military Academy (IMA) over the next four years that shaped a raw, scrappy youngster into a refined personality, sowing the seeds for my future leadership roles in different capacities in the army.

I had obviously been selected to join the army on the basis of certain qualities or leadership attributes that the Selection Board must have observed in me. The training at NDA and IMA not only served to extract and hone these dormant qualities but also imparted new ones that went on to define my character as I assumed a range of challenging roles in the course of my army career.

Today, as I pen down the vital markers of the military leadership mindset that I have imbibed over forty-three years of my military life, entering it as a naïve seventeen-year-old and ending it as a wizened sixty-year-old in January 2022, I can say with certainty that the fire in the belly has not dimmed at all, with my immense reverence and love for the profession still intact. During the course of my long innings, I have commanded men and women from diverse backgrounds, following different languages and cultural practices, and served under bosses (not all of whom can be called 'leaders') of all shapes, sizes and character. The environments and physical conditions I have encountered during these decades have ranged from extreme danger to the leisure of peacetime soldiering, both in India as well as during my various assignments abroad. And I daresay that I may have assimilated every possible leadership style delineated across various leadership manuals, practising them in my life as well, mostly obtrusively, others subconsciously and some with eyes wide open

Leadership: Theories Versus Practical Approach

Before penning down my thoughts on leadership in the military, I thought it prudent to relook at various leadership theories. I must have consciously or inadvertently learnt all these leadership theories or approaches during my training at the NDA and IMA, or later while pursuing some courses of instructions at the Infantry School or the Army War College as a commissioned officer. Honestly speaking, though I do not recollect even a single one of them per se, I must admit that a bit of each of these influenced all my decisions as a military commander during my service, making me emerge as a successful leader.

This rich experience endows me with the ability to understand and share the nuances of some critical leadership theories, as well as how the practical aspects of leadership are notably different from these theories—after all, those implementing these theories are not the ones imparting their lessons while standing on the podium! So, here goes—join me as I take you through various leadership 'theories' versus 'how we do it in the military'.

The *Trait Theory*, also called the *Dispositional Theory*, postulates that successful leadership emerges from certain innate personality traits that lead to consistent behaviour across different situations, and only a person exhibiting those traits can be called a leader. However, I learnt a valuable lesson from the squadron washerman in the NDA that has stayed with me ever since—he ingrained the learning in me that, as a cadet, I should never wear soiled clothes, as that may become a wrong habit, and as an officer of the defence forces, both my dress and demeanour have to be immaculate at all times, fostering unbeatable confidence in myself as a leader.

The *Behavioural Approach*, at times called the *Style Theory*, focuses on what leaders do and how they behave in different situations as opposed to their natural attributes. I was not even aware of this theory until my NDA divisional officer (equivalent to the rank of captain in the army/ lieutenant in the navy/flight lieutenant in the air force) informed me that as a cadet of the NDA, I was mandated to always wear an NDA tie whenever I had to go to Pune town on 'liberty', irrespective of the weather, that is, even in the scorching summers. The explanation offered for this rule was that an NDA cadet must always stand out in a crowd.

The *Situational Approach* lays overriding emphasis on the situation. It posits that a successful leader willingly and efficiently adapts to the dynamics and demands of any situation. Implying that there is no 'one-size-fits-all' leadership style, this flexible approach suggests that leaders can deal with any challenge through a dynamic leadership style that will empower even their employees **and bring out the best in them.** No leadership theory teaches you to pay tributes to your dead enemy or carry the dead body of your buddy on your shoulders for three days without food or water, but in the army, these things are done as an 'honour code' imbibed by a soldier through the period of their service and in the field rather than in a classroom. The aspect of 'honour code' is discussed in detail in the later chapters.

The *Functional Approach* questions the Trait Theory of Leadership, stressing that leadership is the outcome of the interaction among three variables, namely, the leader, the group they are leading and the task in hand. This approach, which entails cumulatively fulfilling the needs of the individual, the team and the mandate, is thus focused on the actions of each group member rather than the behaviour of a single leader. I would like to agree with this theory to the extent that leadership is inclusive rather than exclusive to the team. No leader is bigger than the team; in fact, a leader is as good or as bad as the team itself. When leaders motivate their teams to excel, they are, in the bargain, proving and establishing themselves as leaders. I will go a step further and point out that no leadership theory suggests that the leader's spouse or other family members should also support a leader in his duty; but this is an unwritten honour code for the families in the military. One of the chapters in this book, 'Strong Families Help Build Strong Leaders', is dedicated to the role of families in a soldier's life.

As per the *Transactional Approach*, a leader considers the relationship between him and his subordinates as a transaction, wherein the needs of the subordinates are met if their performance is aligned with the expectations of the leader. In this unique 'quid pro quo' environment, the behaviour of the two parties is seemingly bartered as the followers perceive the leader to be one who will deliver rewards and promotions for their performance. Such an approach may promote highly selfish behaviour if practised in isolation. In the military, on the other hand, the policy of rewards and punishment goes hand in hand with encouraging efficiency and weeding out indiscipline, while ensuring that the image of the organization remains untarnished. I remember an incident where we were caught eating at a local restaurant just outside the IMA premises by a havildar instructor, commonly referred to as 'Ustad' (instructor) by the gentlemen cadets. To extricate ourselves from the tricky situation, we pleaded with the ustad that eating should not be considered an offence. The ustad imbued in us a life lesson in leadership that day when he said that the offence he was charging us for was not eating out without permission but eating at a 'not-an-officer-like place'. He said, *'Agar aap 5-star hotel mein khana kha rahe hote toh main aap ko chhod deta, kyuki woh ek officer-like kaam hai'* (If I had caught you eating in a 5-star hotel, I would have let you off because that would be an officer-like act)!

The ***Transformational Approach*** asserts that leaders ought to aim for 'transforming' others under their charge in the larger interest of the organization. Using this approach, leaders influence others by imparting a sense of identity both to the project in hand as also the company, through a shared vision. They literally walk the talk and lead by example, becoming role models and encouraging others to think for themselves, learn from their mistakes and display creativity and innovativeness in the long run. This attitude enables the leaders to mentor their subordinates and carry them forward in the agenda for progress instead of merely maintaining the status quo. I totally agree with this theory and submit that the essence—that a leader must always be in control of the situation and the team and should be able to influence them—is embodied in the DNA of every leader in the military. This comes not from classroom teachings but from practical experience acquired along with our brothers-in-arms in the field. I also remember my first horse-riding episode in the NDA, with my equitation instructor Subedar Fauja Singh Saab, a tall lanky national-level horse rider, bellowing at me in his commanding voice, 'Cadet, *majboot pakad banao aur kas ke baitho, ghode ko pata lagna chahiye ki uske upar Indian Army ka afsar baitha hua hai*' (Cadet, sit tight with a solid grip, the horse must know that an Indian Army officer is riding him). An army man would also do well to internalize the advice delivered by Bhishma Pitamah to Yudhishthira in the epic Mahabharata, 'A king's first duty is to his people. He should take care of them, with no thoughts of pleasing himself, subordinating his own wishes and desires to those of his people. He should guard them as a mother guards her child.'

In summation, I would say that two common strands that run across each of these definitions are the capability of the leaders to tackle all situations with a positive mindset and their concern for the people for whom they are responsible. Here I must quote Saroj Dutt, our Hindi teacher in Class IX, who counselled us, 'Never think poorly of yourself even in your dreams and not even as a casual joke because the brain picks up the thoughts not knowing if you are serious or not and may portray this as your personality trait at a crucial moment.'

The 'Whats' and 'Whys' of Leadership

Everyone Is a Leader

The word 'leader' is derived from the Anglo-Saxon word, 'laedan', meaning 'to go before as a guide'. The practice of

leadership has been in vogue since the origin of mankind with only the terminology varying across historical contexts. In the olden days, the terms used to describe a leader were 'king', 'chief', 'head' and 'captain', among others. Significantly, the word 'leader' appeared in the English language in AD 1300, but its classification as an amalgam of attributes in the word 'leadership' took another 500 years, appearing in dictionaries only about AD 1800. Notwithstanding this history and evolution of the concept of formal leadership, informally it may be said that each one of us is a leader in some form or the other, leading an entire organization, a team, a group of friends or our family members.

Defining a Leader

The term 'leadership' has been defined in many different ways. Until World War II, most definitions viewed a leader as a key person in any group, imbued with superhuman qualities and single-handedly driving the group towards attainment of the goal(s) it had set for itself. It was only around the middle of the twentieth century that there was a definite shift in this definition, with leadership being perceived as a three-pronged interactive process between the leader, the group and the situation. The *Oxford Dictionary* defines leadership as 'the action of leading a group of people or an organisation'. Further, leadership is an action and not merely a position. It is also not a product of chronological increase in age; as in real life, there is no perfect age for a person to become an effective leader.

Leadership Versus Management

In simple parlance, leaders lead people, whereas managers manage work. While the former signifies a human dimension,

the latter has to do with the optimal utilization of resources. In this sense, leadership can be categorized as an 'art' because leaders have to creatively deal with the dynamic nature of human beings to achieve results, while management is a 'science', with managers performing the functions of planning, organizing, directing and controlling resources to meet goals.

The main difference between leaders and managers thus lies in the process and the resources they use to accomplish their respective missions or objectives. For a more nuanced comparison between the two, the different components of the two processes have been tabulated below.

Mandate of a Leader	Mandate of a Manager
Create vision (a long-term goal)	Create goals (a short-term goal)
Lead people (qualitative)	Manage tasks (quantitative)
Encourage and influence (sell)	Assign tasks and direct (tell)
Establish relationships	Establish systems and processes
Take risks	Minimize risks
Create change (seek feedback)	React to change—maintain or subtly counter the status quo

In an organizational context, regardless of whether a person is designated as a 'manager' or a 'leader', they not only have to optimally manage the resources available to them but also

have to influence their subordinates in a manner so as to obtain their willing obedience, confidence and cooperation to accomplish goals. Hence, both leadership and management are interdependent.

Management without leadership can lead to apathy or lack of motivation among the team members, whereas leadership without management may lead to a disconnect between the leader and the team. Thus, the best leaders are also good managers.

The 'Whys' and 'Hows' of Leadership

As discussed above, the various theories of leadership incorporate a synthesis of behaviours that have been observed, analysed and documented over a period of time. This implies that when one sees an individual engage in a certain behaviour, it enhances one's understanding of the qualities that individual possesses, also providing insights on the prominent characteristics of a leader.

Leadership can also be learnt by 'doing', but this necessitates incisiveness in the persons concerned, who must realize that they have succeeded in attaining the qualities of a leader. Even more important, they must be able to distinguish between varied leadership styles and adapt these to different organizations, different people and different situations. Hence, the felt need and criticality of such a study of leadership, which equips prospective learners with the toolkit to deal with diverse challenges at both the personal and professional levels.

I also humbly wish to point out that all my readers are likely distinguished young leaders in their respective communities and could go on to occupy professional positions of high authority in future. Hence, this study of leadership will act as a guide for them to gainfully use the learning in their spheres of influence.

Modern Leadership Challenges

Automation Versus Leadership

It is perceived that by 2030, almost 50 per cent of all work will be automated. However, notwithstanding technological developments, human leaders will still remain the driving force for driving positive change in an organization. In the evolving workspace, leaders can increasingly delegate many routine managerial and monotonous functions to artificial intelligence (AI) and shift their focus to other important areas of work, such as innovation, strategy, optimizing employee productivity and out-of-the-box solutions for common challenges.

Intergenerational Workforce

With age becoming just a number, the seventies is the new fifties today. Thus, in the workplace, leaders may have multiple generations working under them, including highly tech-savvy millennial kids, social media influencers, inspirational achievers and ambitious job-hoppers in their middle age, in contrast to the erstwhile corporate ecosystem with little diversity, wherein individuals usually stuck to one job and one workplace throughout their careers. An efficient boss needs to understand and respond to the needs and aspirations of all the diverse workers engaged at the workplace, to maximize their strengths and navigate through their weaknesses, while ensuring an appropriate mix of tradition with modernity.

Hybrid Working

This entails implementation of a flexible work model comprising a mix of in-office and at-home or remote functioning, especially in post-COVID times. In this context, leaders need to know how to effectively manage their remote teams, lay down clear expectations, organize virtual meetings and ensure accountability and regular communication among their team members. Most importantly, they must know how to identify and deal with the social isolation and digital exhaustion that may creep in within the workforce.

Cultural Diversity and Gender Sensitivity

This is one aspect wherein military forces win hands down. Learning lessons from the latter, all organizations and leaders need to foster gender-sensitive, fair and non-discriminatory policies of inclusiveness.

Employee Well-Being

Technology can facilitate work, but constant exposure to it could also have adverse impacts on the human psyche, leading to loneliness, screen stress and mental health issues, which, in turn, negatively affect performance and productivity. Ensuring good working conditions, occupational health support, conflict and stress management, viable social interactions and leading by example are a few things that army officers practise as a matter of routine, especially during field postings in combat areas characterized by greater danger and uncertainty.

Attributes of an Effective Leader

Global views on what qualities make one an effective leader are very diverse; most of them reflect personal experiences and styles that have helped leaders achieve success in their own professional lives. Moreover, the jargon used today to describe these attributes is also quite different from what members of the 'baby boomer' generation were taught. However, most of these qualities can still be subsumed under one head—for instance, the 'art of articulation', 'getting the message across' or 'clarity of intent communicated to subordinates' may be collectively clubbed under 'communication skills'.

I have culled out the following key attributes that are relevant for dealing with the challenges of modern leadership, which are largely based on my long and varied experience in the field.

Professional Competence

This is the **soul and sine qua non** of leadership. This aspect was first conveyed to me by my first commanding officer (CO), Brigadier (then Lt Col) Trigunesh Mukherjee during my first interview with him on my commissioning as second lieutenant in the battalion. After the initial niceties and the interview were done and dusted, he told me in his unique style (pardon the language), 'If you are in touch with your profession, no son of a b**ch can touch you.' Professional competence is thus a function of the knowledge gained through hard work and its upgradation is a continuous process. However, let us not mix things here—it is quite another thing to be well-qualified and knowledgeable. Remember, there are some things one cannot fake for long—Courage, Compassion, Commitment, Creativity, Competence and last but not least, Character.

Integrity

Integrity essentially signifies high moral value and is the most essential ingredient of each component of the triumvirate of *Wafadari, Imaandari, Zimmedari* (**Loyalty, Honesty, Responsibility**). Good leaders walk the talk and talk only the talk, ensuring that they are doing the right thing, even when no one is watching.

Vision

This implies the ability to see the big picture, also encompassing foresight. It imparts a sense of purpose to the team and motivates them to achieve the set goals. Remember that 'Leadership without vision is just management'.

Endurance

This is both physical and mental, as it represents the ability to withstand hardship, adversity and stress. It is tantamount to a self-motivating dynamic ability to slug it out with one's team in the field or the boardroom. More than the ability to bear difficulty, it presupposes the willingness and motivation to turn that difficulty into glory, to convert failure into success. The 'Commando Course' in the Indian Army is a thirty-three-day long training, considered to be the toughest military course in the world. Having attended this course myself, I can say that after the successful completion of this course, I realized not only the extremes of physical hardship that my body was capable of enduring but, more importantly, the mental strength that led my mind to command my body to withstand the utter physical and mental stress.

Humility

The army also taught me that a leader needs to accept mistakes with humility, as, in the army, any arrogance on the part of the leader can endanger lives. It is also important for a leader to be a good listener who values feedback, which is vital for the organization's growth.

Spirituality

This is suggestive of a faith and connectivity with a higher power, which is not to be confused with religion or a set of organized beliefs and practices. Spirituality helps a leader achieve 'self-actualization' and realize one's true potential to achieve an 'ideal self' or a better version of oneself. It also allows the leader to see the good in others, distinguish right from wrong and help one better deal with stress and adversity. A highly recommended path to spirituality is meditation, which helps in the release of the chemical called serotonin that helps one experience bliss and happiness.

Apart from the main attributes mentioned above, some of the other primary aspects of a leader's persona include decisiveness, empathy, anticipation, composure and humour. The popular adage, 'To handle yourself, use your head; to handle others, use your heart', echoes the importance of empathy and concern in a leader's mind. It refers to the emotional quotient of a leader, which builds trust and confidence. Further, demeanour is more important than deportment. Self-control, especially in adverse situations, is the hallmark of the inner strength of a leader. Leaders also need to imbibe the ability to stand up for their convictions and travel the road less travelled. In addition, they should cultivate the courage to stand and speak up for

their convictions, or to sit down and listen to others with compassion and caring. Finally, exhibiting a subtle sense of humour, especially when things are not going your way, is a fascinating trait. The analogy that 'a person without a sense of humour is like a wagon without springs, which is jolted by every pebble on the road' is quite apt for defining a leader's disposition. A Harvard Study also finds that 'leaders with humour are 27 per cent more admired than the average, and their teams are 15 per cent more committed'.[1]

What Motivates a Soldier to Make the Supreme Sacrifice in the Line of Duty?

Having spent the better part of my life in the army, I cannot overlook this highly very emotive but most central aspect of every soldier's life, which is their unwavering commitment to duty, which is related to 'combat leadership'. In the following section, I would like to take you through the military, emotional and social environment and challenges under which a soldier functions and still *decides to shine the way they shine.* The intention here is not to draw a comparison between the soldier and their civilian counterparts but to provide an overview of some of the best practices of the armed forces, which may also be replicated in the corporate world and civilian organizations.

Nation First

On joining the armed forces, every soldier takes the oath of duty and sacrifice that the interest of the country is supreme, and that the nation will always come first. This is almost a

---

[1] Source: David Reyero, 'Sense of humour. An underestimated leadership skill?', Do Better, 22 April 2022, https://dobetter.esade.edu/en/professional-sense-humor.

sacred bond between the Individual and the State, reflected in the Chetwode Motto, as delineated below:

Chetwode Motto

**The safety, honour and welfare of the country
come first, always and every time.
The honour, welfare and comfort of the men you
command come next.
Your own ease, comfort and safety come last,
always and every time.**

This motto is etched on the walls of Chetwode Hall in the IMA, Dehradun, into which the gentlemen cadets (nowadays referred to in a gender-neutral way as 'officer cadets') march, after passing out of the IMA as commissioned officers. This motto is *the sum and substance of the approach to soldiering for Indian Army officers.*

Education and Training

The concept of a 'scholar soldier' entails imparting the requisite military skills to a soldier, not only equipping them with the ability to deal with any battle but also enhancing their self-worth and motivation. All soldiers have to go through rigorous, structured, progressive and experiential training at each stage of service, as young, middle and senior-level officers or jawans/junior commissioned officers (JCOs). 'The more you train in peace, the less you bleed in war' is an oft-repeated saying in the Indian Army.

Naam, Namak, Nishan

This is another triumvirate of the Indian Army, signifying a core honour code that drives the soldier and provides them inspiration and motivation. It is discussed in detail in the subsequent chapters.

The *Paltan* Is One's Mother

The terms 'unit', 'battalion', 'regiment' or *paltan*, often used interchangeably, refer to a cohesive entity of soldiers who train and fight under one name, one loyalty and one flag. The commanding officer (who is invariably of the rank of a colonel or lieutenant colonel), respectfully referred to as 'CO Saab', is the head of a unit. Every soldier fights for the *Paltan ki Izzat* (honour of the paltan or unit), ready to lay down their life for upholding that honour, which means that they are actually fighting for the army, and again by implication, the nation. The sentiment evoked here is the same as if one were fighting to protect the honour of one's mother or family name. 'I will never let down my comrades' is also an unwritten emotional bond amongst the soldiers, and between the soldiers and leaders. This attitude is enacted not only in battle but also on the sports field, where some of the most ferocious and intense 'battles' have taken place for protecting the pride of the unit.

Faith in God

As discussed above, spiritual well-being imparts psychological strength to a soldier. The beliefs of every soldier are accommodated, founded on the secular ethos of the armed forces. Irrespective of the personal religious beliefs or faiths of individuals, all members of the entire unit pray together and the faith of the soldiers becomes the faith of the officers.

Whole of the Family Approach

Everyone has heard the phrase, 'the Whole of the Nation Approach'. However, when a soldier joins the unit, they, in a sense, join a new family, a large family comprising their fellow soldiers, seniors and spouses, children and parents of the comrades. The officers in charge are responsible not only for the soldier's well-being but also that of their families. This imparts confidence and assurance to the soldier that they have a family at the workplace and that their biological family will be cared for and looked after, even if and when they are not there.

Patriotism

This umbrella concept symbolizes 'Pride in Uniform' or the profound motivation for a soldier, which is enshrined in the Constitution and reinforced by the fact that the country recognizes their services, and the common citizenry knows that the soldier is the last bastion of hope in case of any danger to them or their country

Age Is No Bar for You to Shine

The following instances suggest that a leader can display exemplary leadership at any age and stage in their life.

- In 1675, at the age of nine, Sri Guru Gobind Singh ji was formally installed as the leader of the Sikhs after his father Sri Guru Tegh Bahadur was executed by the Mughal Emperor Aurangzeb.

- In 1646, sixteen-year-old Chhatrapati Shivaji Maharaj captured Torna Fort and seized the large treasure found there.
- Maharaja Ranjit Singh of the Sikh Empire fought in his first battle when he was only ten years old. And at the age of seventeen, he succeeded in halting the King of Afghanistan, Zaman Shah Durrani's invasion of India.
- Honorary Captain (Subedar Major) Yogendra Singh Yadav, being the youngest recipient of the Param Vir Chakra at the age of nineteen years, exhibited extraordinary courage during the Kargil War. Despite being shot fifteen times, he led the assault that captured Tiger Hill, a pivotal moment in the conflict.
- Rao Abdul Hafiz Khan was the youngest (at eighteen years and five months) Indian recipient of the Victoria Cross, the highest and most prestigious award for gallantry in the face of the enemy that can be awarded to British and Commonwealth forces.
- Suhas Gopinath, CEO and chairman of Global Inc., is the youngest CEO in the world, at the age of only seventeen years.
- Colonel Harland Sanders was sixty-two years of age when he first franchised Kentucky Fried Chicken (KFC).
- Yuichiro Miura of Japan scaled Mount Everest at the age of eighty.
- Kaamya Karthikeyan is the youngest Indian to climb Mount Everest, having achieved this feat at the age of sixteen.

- Teghbir Singh, a five-year-old boy from Ropar, Punjab, is the youngest Asian to climb Mount Kilimanjaro in Africa. He reached the summit of Uhuru Peak, the mountain's highest point, on 23 August 2024.
- Last but not least, just to make it a bit lighter, let me indulge in some self-praise: Lt Gen. K.J.S. 'Tiny' Dhillon authored his maiden national bestselling book at the age of sixty-one, undertook his first modelling assignment at the age of sixty-two, wrote his second book and acted in a documentary film at the age of sixty-three.

I conclude this chapter with one of the most eloquent descriptions of a soldier's life—an apt illustration of what shines in him:

> *'The soldier is the army. No army is better than its soldiers. The soldier is also a citizen. In fact, the highest obligation and privilege of citizenship is that of bearing arms for one's country.'*
> —General George S. Patton Jr, US Army

2

Wafadari, Imaandari, Zimmedari (Loyalty, Integrity, Responsibility)

निषेवते प्रशस्तानि निन्दितानि न सेवते अनास्तिक:
श्रद्धा एतद् राजर्शिन: लक्षणम्

*'The wise are those who adhere to their duties, who stand
by their words, who praise the deserving, criticize the
undeserving, who are untouched by selfish interest and
who are revered for their virtues. Such people deserve the
position of leadership.'*

The Values That Define Our Lives

Every soldier of the Indian Army/Indian Defence Forces
lives and dies by two basic tenets of the military ethos that
guide them through their service career. These are '**Naam,
Namak, Nishan**' and '**Wafadari, Imaandari, Zimmedari**',
which can be described as follows:

Naam, Namak, Nishan

Naam: Legacy or reputation of your unit/regiment; popularly
known as *paltan ki izzat* (honour and pride of the regiment/
unit), implying that a soldier is always ready to lay down their
life for the sake of upholding the paltan's izzat.

Namak: Allegiance to the salt you have partaken as a member of your unit/regiment/army/nation. A common adage in India that states, *'Jiska namak khaya ho, uske saath be-imaani nahi kar sakte'* (You cannot be dishonest with someone whose salt you have eaten), is steeped in the nation's cultural ethos, which perceives any betrayal of the person who feeds you as the ultimate sacrilege.

Nishan: The Indian Army carries the flag of the regiment on every battlefield, with the insignia or colours on the flag acting not only as a motivating factor for the troops but also a reminder that it would be the ultimate ignominy were the enemy to seize their regiment colours. Every soldier thus fights for the nishan (the flag or colours of his regiment). This symbolism of protection and respect for the nation's honour has often been depicted in Indian cinema, where dying soldiers refuse to let the flag they are carrying droop to the ground even when they are being decimated by enemy fire. It is therefore no exaggeration to say that an Indian soldier always adheres to the honour code of Naam, Namak, Nishan, protecting the nishan (flag) throughout their life, and if accosted by death, they proudly come back home wrapped in the same nishan or national flag.

Wafadari, Imaandari, Zimmedari

The terms 'Wafadari', 'Imaandari' and 'Zimmedari' signify another triad that also stays with an Indian soldier through life and death. The words, standing for Loyalty, Honesty and Responsibility, respectively, constitute the cornerstone of a soldier's character and behaviour. A soldier's life is always full of challenges, both professional and personal, as their career has a significant impact on the well-being of their family throughout their service in the defence forces and even

beyond. It is this resilience and never-say-die spirit espoused and exhibited by an Indian soldier that ensures victory even in the face of heavy odds. The army is not a profession but a bonding for life.

Here I would like to share a quote from my first book, *Kitne Ghazi Aaye, Kitne Ghazi Gaye*:

> This is also what I told a student in Gujarat University, who asked me a question at an interactive session during my recent visit to Ahmedabad, 'Sir, how challenging is an army job?' My spontaneous and honest reply was, 'Army *ek* job *nahin hai, mohabbat hai. Aur mohabbat mein* challenges *nahin hote, afsaane hote hain'* (Being in the army is not a job, it is like an unending love affair, and in love there are only legends, not challenges).'

An army officer's actions should always be above board, beyond any kind of suspicion, and aimed at protecting the best interests of all they are responsible for, including the jawans, and above all, the nation.

This unwritten bond of trust and allegiance to the forces and the country encompasses not only the soldiers or officers who have taken an oath to lay down their lives in the line of duty but also their spouses and families, who often display exemplary courage and sacrifice, standing shoulder to shoulder with their spouses, children and siblings in the face of any challenge or adversity. Here, it is important to highlight the invaluable contribution of the soldiers' families, especially their spouses, which is seldom acknowledged, leave aside appreciated or celebrated, but which is the critical succour for those who daringly venture into battle. The story of my life too is peppered with similar instances of sacrifice and valour exhibited by my wife, who faced at least two traumatic occasions when she heard of my purported 'death', or rather news of my death, in the media, once when she was in the eighth month of pregnancy. These instances have also been detailed in my earlier book.

Among the triad, Wafadari, Imaandari and Zimmedari, the concept of Zimmedari, or responsibility, as practised by members of the Indian Army, goes far beyond its literal dictionary meaning.

Duty Versus Zimmedari

The words 'duty' and 'responsibility' are ostensibly synonymous in meaning, but there is a huge difference in their perceived meanings when applied to the heart and mind of an Indian soldier. The difference between the two is also reflected in seemingly small but meaningful gestures. I would like to cite here an example of a video gone viral on social media, showing an auto driver dropping off a schoolgirl at her destination. The driver's duty was confined to dropping the girl at the appointed place and driving off. However, he goes beyond the call of duty, deciding to wait until he is assured that the girl has reached her home safely. This decision to wait for extra time to ensure his passenger's safety transforms the auto driver's duty into zimmedari, as performed by a responsible citizen. In the same vein, if each of us goes the extra mile to deliver our responsibility instead of merely performing our routine duties, we would definitely be able to create a more amenable and empathetic society, making the world a better place to live in. It is this commitment towards zimmedari that defines the culture of the Indian Army, which also imbues a special place of pride for it at the national level. Another conspicuous example of such responsibility at the

international level is that of Japanese fans who meticulously clean up the stands before leaving a football stadium even if their team has lost the game, leaving them disappointed and distraught.

Coming back to my personal life, I recall another instance in 2015 when I was posted in Delhi. My wife Nita was returning from Gurgaon (now Gurugram) to Delhi Cantonment in our private car. On the way, at the Mahipalpur flyover, she saw a twenty-four or twenty-five-year-old youth lying on the road near his motorcycle bleeding, having met with a serious accident. Although a motley crowd of more than fifty-odd people had gathered around him, none of them came forward to help the injured young man. Aghast, Nita immediately stepped up to help, transferring the young man into her car with the help of the driver and taking him to the emergency ward of the army hospital. At the hospital, everybody advised her to back off, suggesting that she would get into trouble with the police questioning her, followed by numerous court appearances to give evidence about the accident, but Nita ignored all such suggestions, steadfast in her resolve to help a fellow citizen, come what may. And sure enough, when the police arrived at the hospital, they did not ask her or me even a single question because as per the law, anyone who helps an injured person and brings them to the hospital cannot be questioned. Unfortunately, the young man lost his life due to excessive bleeding, but Nita's determination to help a human being in distress when others failed to do so is a manifestation of the real zimmedari of a conscientious citizen. If we collectively imbibe such a quality, there is no reason why we cannot build India into a great nation, and the training provided by the army shows us the way.

That is the concept of zimmedari—when you act beyond the call of your duty or what you are supposed to do or what you are paid to do.

Commitment Versus Wafadari

As military commanders, we are bound by an honour code of loyalty (wafadari) and commitment to ensure the well-being of the officers and soldiers under our command. Here, I am reminded of another incident when as a brigadier, I was commanding a Rashtriya Rifles (RR) sector in the jungles of Rajwar and Haphruda in North Kashmir. We had launched a massive counterterrorist operation, wherein more than 1000 troops had been carrying out swarming operations in the jungles of Rajwar for over a month. As the sector commander, I was personally monitoring the operation, leading my men from the forward-most RR post, which was about an hour's drive from my sector headquarters. I had stationed myself at the post so that I could be available at the site for guiding the men or giving instructions in case of any emergency or if the need for additional troops arose. Coincidentally, my wife Nita, her mother and our daughter had come to Kashmir to visit me around the same time. But since I was away on the call of duty, the three of them stayed put at the sector headquarters, waiting for me to return from the operation after four days. Since I did not want to return to the sector headquarters and abandon my men at the post to deal with any unforeseen crisis or avoidable casualties, I had to ignore the presence of my family, who had come especially to spend some time with me. As per service norms, it would have been absolutely in order for me to have returned to the sector headquarters for a few hours and rejoined the operations later. But for me, as the leader of the operation, the wafadari and

commitment towards my troops was supremely important, and I could not ignore the safety of my men over my personal responsibility towards my family. Further, I felt it prudent to be continuously present at the site of the operation so that I could take well-informed decisions depending upon the dynamic situation. This wafadari towards my soldiers and their families, overriding my commitment towards my own family, is the essence of the ethos of military leadership that has been instilled in us since our inception into the army, the ethos of leading from the front with utter disregard for personal safety and comfort to ensure the safety and well-being of the troops we command, always and every time. This military honour code of wafadari need not remain confined to the forces and can be imbibed by every individual in a team at the workplace or as a responsible member of society to build a better organization or country.

In the context of wafadari in a soldier's life, I would like to narrate another incident that occurred in the jungles of North Kashmir when I was commanding the Chinar Corps there during 2019–20. A counterterrorist operation was underway in the dense forests close to the Line of Control (LoC) after an infiltrating group of terrorists had been intercepted there. Additional Special Forces (SF) troops were also inducted to reinforce the teams in contact with the infiltrators. During the operation, one of the SF officers was hit by a volley of terrorist bullets, leaving him bleeding profusely with gunshot wounds and shattered bones. A young doctor who had recently joined the RR unit in Kashmir accompanying the team was immediately summoned to the site where the injured officer was lying. The doctor, who had probably never seen such a grievous injury earlier in his life, was stunned and almost went numb. The

JCO, second-in-charge of the party, who was now heading the team, was a seasoned soldier with more than twenty-five years of service and a veteran of many such operations. He immediately sensed the situation and pacified the doctor, calmly reminding him of his professional ethics and wafadari beyond his own fears and apprehensions.

The young doctor regained his composure but realized that he was not carrying splints needed to externally bind the wounded limb. These splints act as a stabilizing frame to hold the broken bones in the proper position so the patient can be evacuated over a short distance with ease and comfort. The doctor knew that without splints, it would be difficult for such a seriously injured person to withstand evacuation out of the jungle to the nearest roadhead where an ambulance could transport him to a helipad site for further evacuation by air. Thinking on his feet, the young doctor gathered some branches from the trees around to secure the limb properly and the evacuation began. When I visited the 92 Base Hospital in the evening to meet the patients, I was told by the hospital commandant that the most unorthodox and yet professional use of locally made splints, beyond what is taught in medical colleges, had actually saved the life of this officer. Overwhelmed, I complimented the young doctor for overcoming his personal trauma and innovatively and imaginatively using local resources to save the life of a fellow soldier. The Indian Army is, in fact, full of such examples wherein soldiers and officers have saved each other's lives by going beyond the charted path, which is what I mean by wafadari beyond commitment.

Obligation Versus Imaandari

The core values of honesty and integrity in a soldier's life are non-negotiable and the importance of discipline cannot

be overemphasized. Performing one's duty is an obligation conferred upon us by the law of the land and the rules of the organization we serve. Hence, every employee in the corporate sector is supposed to do their assigned job to the best of their abilities as per the needs or the demands of the organization. However, there is a possibility that the employee will not exhibit 100 per cent honesty, commitment or obligation towards the job. In contrast, a soldier, especially a commander, does not enjoy the luxury of just accomplishing the assigned task as an obligation because in the military, the actions of one individual may result in their buddy or themselves losing their life or a failed mission, resulting in national disgrace or a calamity.

On another occasion, when I was an RR sector commander in North Kashmir, a massive search and destroy operation was being carried out in the jungles very close to the LoC. It was a time-consuming and highly tedious operation in extremely difficult and inhospitable terrain and weather. Since the operation was getting prolonged beyond a reasonable time frame, I had to arrange for additional fresh troops to maintain the tempo of the operations. This included a platoon comprising approximately thirty soldiers of specialized troops from an RR battalion operating under a young captain, which was deployed with other integral troops of my sector in the jungle. The young captain, full of enthusiasm, was keen to achieve success for his team and his unit. Since I had operated in that area as a youngster, I was fully conversant with the ground conditions. After we had attained some successes close to the general area of deployment of this platoon, I ordered the specialized platoon to be relocated to a comparatively non-active area in a re-entrant or low ground between two hill spurs in the jungle. Assuming that by moving his troops away from the main action to ensure success only for the integral troops of my sector, the captain, who was desperate to achieve success in the operation, called up his commanding officer who was stationed more than 250 km away and shared his apprehensions. Incidentally, the commanding officer was well known to me and fully aware of my style of command as he had served with me during an earlier tenure. So, he urged the captain not to doubt my intentions, firmly telling him to have faith in the judgement of 'Brigadier Tiny Dhillon' (that is, me), and obey his orders as his honesty of purpose could not be questioned. Consequently, the young officer, albeit reluctantly but maintaining surprise with full tactical manoeuvres, moved his team to the designated location. Within two hours of the deployment of his team at the new location, they cited two terrorists, engaging them with fire. After a short firefight, the specialized platoon managed to eliminate the terrorists, thereby achieving success for their team and the unit.

After his team was relieved from the operation, the officer travelled with me in my vehicle from the operations area to my headquarters. On the way, he was honest enough to narrate the entire incident to me, also telling me about the persistence of his doubts regarding my orders despite his commanding officer telling him, in no uncertain terms, about the honesty of purpose always displayed by 'Brigadier Tiny Dhillon'. He was sitting on the rear seat of the vehicle, so I turned my head towards him from my seat in the front and simply smiled at him. Then I asked him if he really wanted to know why he had been relocated to a completely unknown location away from the main operations site. When he nodded in the affirmative, I told him that since I had operated in the same area as a youngster many years ago,

I was aware of the only water spring in this area where the terrorists, surrounded by our forces, would come to fetch water. I had therefore relocated his team next to that spring but did not want to convey the real reason for my decision over the radio set for the sake of maintaining confidentiality. And sure enough, as I had expected, the terrorists came down to the spring to collect water, making it easy for his team to neutralize them.

Humbled by my revelation, the captain acknowledged that his doubts about my intention were misplaced. More importantly, he asserted that the key lesson he had learnt from this incident was that the top priority for any commander or leader is always to accomplish the mission assigned to him without compromising the safety of his troops, as that is a non-negotiable component in his charter of duties. When I reminisced about this incident later, it reinforced what was already clear to me—that the obligation to perform one's assigned task may be well understood but accomplishing it with 100 per cent commitment and honesty of purpose is actually a delineation of the imaandari that military training imparts in the soldiers. Just merely accomplishing your mandated obligations is not good enough unless the honesty of purpose (imaandari) brings that additional non-negotiable flavour to your success. This ethos has always stayed with me, subconsciously guiding my actions even away from the combat zone.

I would like to narrate another incident highlighting this honesty of purpose beyond the mandatory obligation of performing a duty, displayed by a young woman officer when I was the Chinar Corps commander in Kashmir. A corps headquarters is characterized by the presence of different departments dealing with various aspects, including operations, intelligence, logistics, administration, media, civil military liaison and discipline, among others, which are manned by officers of varying ranks and seniority. These officers would report to me, regularly briefing me about the progress related to the respective matters they were dealing with. One of the departments in the corps headquarters, known as the discipline and vigilance (DV) department, basically deals with complaints and other disciplinary aspects involving allegations levelled against military personnel pertaining to their personal character or military reputation. Being highly sensitive issues, they have to be tackled with great responsibility and confidentiality. As the corps commander, I used to discuss all aspects, other than DV matters, in the operations room in the presence of all the staff officers of the headquarters. However, for the DV cases, I used to call the dealing officer to discuss the issue in the privacy of my office. A highly efficient woman officer, aged about twenty-five to twenty-eight years and qualified in law, who was posted in the DV branch of the corps headquarters, would often come to brief me in the corps commander's office. She would sit across the table, explaining all the sensitive cases in great, at times embarrassing, detail, which any other young lady may have felt recalcitrant to discuss with a man twice her age. But the daring young officer never hesitated to recount even the most intricate details of the complaint and the official staff comments on it to enable me to understand the case in its totality.

One day, I was informally discussing routine matters with a group of officers at a farewell tea party on the lawns of the corps headquarters, where the woman officer in question was also present and engaged in a conversation with me. I ventured to ask her how she could rustle up

the confidence and courage to explain all the cases to me without any hesitation. She candidly replied that if she had not explained the intricacies and finer points of the cases to me, I would not have been able to make a correct decision, which would be akin to not only flouting the principles of natural justice but could also lead to miscarriage of justice, thereby adversely affecting all the concerned parties. It was thus her duty coupled with honesty of purpose beyond the obligation of reporting to me, to clearly state all the facts and ensure the delivery of appropriate justice in accordance with the law. This is yet another instance of imaandari beyond one's obligations which defines military culture and, in my opinion, ought to be emulated even in civilian life.

Regimentation

The *Collins Dictionary* defines 'regimentation' as 'very strict control over the way a group of people behave or the way something is done'. Field Marshal S.H.F.J. Manekshaw, Military Cross, once remarked, 'If anyone tells you he is never afraid, he is a liar or he is a Gorkha.' Similar sentiments have been expressed by officers, JCOs and soldiers about their respective regiments, wherein the spirit of camaraderie, esprit de corps, brothers in arms and above all, solidarity, works as the single-most important factor that unites the officers of the Indian Army in their agenda to win a battle. The regimentation in the army is not merely restricted to soldiers and victory in a battle but also transcends the daily chores within the regiment/group/organization. When a young officer or soldier joins the unit as a greenhorn, they, on the one hand, are trained, motivated, moulded and chiselled into a very sharp combat expert, while, on the other, they are shaped and polished into a very suave, cultured and ethical member of the regiment or unit. Regimentation lasts longer and beyond one's service in uniform and as the adage goes, 'the soldier carries the regimentation with him to his grave'. In most righteous units, the regimentation is invariably carried forward in letter and spirit by the next generation, irrespective of whether they don the uniform or not. I have personally known five generations of some officers and continue to be in touch with the children and grandchildren of most of my regimental officers.

Regimentation is, in fact, not limited to the officers and soldiers of one's own regiment but signifies an emotion that stitches a band of soldiers together with an invisible but unbreakable thread. I had served with an officer from another service many years ago. We never met in person after that but remained virtually in touch with each other, exchanging New Year and festive greetings. After many years of having gone our own ways in the army, when I was posted in Delhi, I received a call from this officer asking me to help his daughter who was visiting Delhi for the first time and was stuck near the Income Tax Office crossing in Delhi with some issue. I immediately contacted the girl whom I had seen long ago when she was a toddler and brought her to the Officers' Mess in Delhi Cantonment. Upon reaching the Mess, I called up her father, but was told by his PA that he was busy in a meeting and would call back later. The girl got really upset, believing that her father was not bothered about her well-being, refusing to even take a call relating to her even if it may well have been another distress call. Despite my attempts to pacify her, the girl continued to be upset with her father's behaviour, clearly expressing her anger when he

did call her back. In his defence, her father, who had not met me or spoken to me over the last two decades, told her that once he had requested Tiny to help her, there was no reason for him to be worried, thus assuaging his daughter's feelings by defining the very spirit of regimentation, which goes beyond a single regiment or unit, encompassing the entire army in its fold. Therefore, the spirit of regimentation in the army symbolizes much more than the 'very strict control' as defined in the *Collins Dictionary*, nor is it merely an order or rule; it's actually a way of life in the defence forces. Regimentation inspires people to go beyond their physical abilities to deliver unparalleled support on and beyond the battlefield.

Talking about regimentation as a way of life in the army, I am reminded of something a very dear friend once told me, who not only gave me the moniker of 'God's favourite child', as mentioned in the last chapter of my first book but also movingly said, 'People join the army as a profession; but you celebrated it like a festival! One can sense it from your books and your personality.'

The renowned motivational speaker Wayne Dyer and the legendary Chinese philosopher Lao Tzu are both credited with similar quotes, broadly accentuating the action of being 'connected to everything but attached to nothing'. I would also like to add a soldier's perspective to this suggestion, emphasizing that human beings are social animals who are born to connect, and this attachment cannot merely be viewed as a materialistic association. Such an attachment can stem from the values of kinship, love, faith, trust, honesty, loyalty, justice, courage, integrity and, above all, the honour code to live and die for the flag.

One of the most important aspects of regimentation is to accept one's mistakes or deficiencies and work diligently to overcome them in order to be a constructive member of any group. As I mentioned earlier, the process of chiselling, moulding, scrubbing, polishing, buffing and finally shining that a new recruit is subjected to will be fully successful only if the person concerned is willing to accept this rigorous training and be mentored.

It is apt to conclude this chapter with the following quotation from one of the most courageous soldiers that India has ever known:

'One individual may die for an idea, but that idea will, after his death, incarnate itself in a thousand lives.'
—Netaji Subhas Chandra Bose

3

The Essence of a
Leader

निश्चित्य य: प्रक्रमते नान्तर्वसति कर्मण :|
अवन्ध्य कालो वश्यात्मा स वै राजर्शि: उच्यते ॥

*'They who, once having commenced a task, keep striving
and never stop until it has been achieved, who seldom
waste their time brooding, and who have their mind
under their control, are undoubtedly wise persons.'*

What Makes a Leader?

Who can be called a leader and how are leaders different from managers, chief executive officers (CEOs), directors or even military commanders? The answer to this basic question pertains to the core definition of a military leadership ethos and its application in civil society. In the simplest terms, if a manager manages, a director directs, a CEO executes the assigned tasks and a military commander commands troops, a leader then is obviously someone who leads. But the essence of the word goes much deeper, for leadership cannot be earned through an appointment letter obtained post an interview or exam, nor does it signify merely a promotion to a higher position in a hierarchy based on performance. Leadership is also not the implementation of a nine-to-five job routine or a

part-time responsibility that one may bear in one's free time. Thus, we can say that there are managers, CEOs, directors and commanders; and then there are leaders, even if they may fall under any of these categories, who personify much more than what these designations may convey.

Leaders Command with Empathy and Authority

Leadership is not a technical attribute or even a science but is actually an art, demanding certain inherent values and traits that create a special vibe and resonate with the people under the command of the leader. Thus, leaders are not born nor can they be fully trained but, like a diamond created by nature under intense heat and pressure, leaders emerge after being honed under extraordinary circumstances combined with focused training and critical skills that can be further sharpened by on-the-job training and experience. While both age and experience are vital for becoming an efficient leader, it is personal charisma that inspires trust among those who follow the leader. The two crucial differences between a leader and a manager or CEO are, firstly, that the former earns trust while the latter may demand it, and secondly, that leaders accept full responsibility for the actions of even the people under their command, whereas managers or CEOs may demand accountability from their subordinates. As a military commander who commanded soldiers in action in the combat zone, I can say with the utmost conviction that the military leadership ethos flows from the concern for the men and women you command and culminates in the successful accomplishment of the mission, which by all accounts, is non-negotiable. Another term prevalent in the corporate world is 'boss'. Here too, there is a conspicuous difference between a leader and a boss. The dictionary defines a boss as

'a person who is in charge of a worker, group, or organisation' and 'gives (someone) orders in a domineering manner', which does not necessarily apply to a leader. However, I can say from personal experience that as the head of a team, I would any day prefer to be called a leader than a boss.

Leaders Are Eternal Learners

Another aspect that is associated with leadership is 'experience vis-à-vis qualifications or education'. Does a better qualified or educated person make a better or more experienced leader? Here, I would like to clarify my understanding of qualifications, which often implies one or more formal degrees earned after having passed a certain examination. Education, on the other hand, represents the values that one learns and imbibes from one's parents, teachers, peers, seniors, juniors, day-to-day dealings with people and from the surroundings that one grows up in. Hence, a person may well be highly qualified but still not well groomed, who is capable of discerning good from bad. Coming back to the debate on experience versus qualifications or education, leaders mature with experience while their qualifications and education act as the foundation pillars for their mental development. As a young second lieutenant, for decision-making, I depended more on the advice of my junior commissioned officers (JCOs) and non-commissioned officers (NCOs) rather than on my own qualifications. Even after gaining substantial experience with the passage of time, I still depended extensively on the practical advice rendered by the JCOs and NCOs because they always operated at the ground level and could gauge the situation from a very tactical viewpoint. Similarly, in a corporate scenario, a CEO may be a highly qualified individual but would not have the experience or insights of the person actually operating the machine on the factory floor. Hence, for successful decision-making, a leader needs to imbibe a healthy mix of experience and knowledge, on the one hand, supplemented by suggestions and innovative ideas from the ground-level staff, on the other. Add to this the qualities of diligence, personal and professional integrity, courage of conviction, creativity and respect for the honour and growth of the men and women you command, and you have a true leader in every sense of the word. It would also be apt to say that a leader's qualification is less important than how they utilize this knowledge to realize the objectives they are working towards achieving.

Leaders Are Humble

A true leader faces failures like a man and success like a gentleman. This statement, however, does not relate only to a specific gender, it is equally relevant to all those in the position of power and responsibility. While humility is a critical attribute among winners, leaders also need to know the strength of their own character. This is especially applicable in the military where a leader's decisions can signify the difference between national glory and military disgrace. Leaders must also remember that winning is largely an outcome of their team's energies, whereas a lack of success may not always imply the absence of earnestness in effort. At the same time, even when you are not successful, you must know that at the end of the day, you may not be half as bad as people will make you out to be. So, just remain focused on your goals, ignoring all the noises around you.

Leaders Are Humane

Identifying a leader from amongst a plethora of CEOs, managers, directors or commanders is a function of the heart more than that of the eyes. This is because leadership is not a title or a position; it's more of a belief emanating from

the heart and soul rather than the eyes. A humane leader understands the strengths and weaknesses of others, steering them towards a common goal for actualizing a broader vision.

What Do Leaders Do?

Leadership: Where Little Things Are Big Things

My experience of nearly four decades in the military, wherein I worked with leaders of varying hierarchies, taught me that the traits needed for leadership are common across all fields of life, with only the team, goals and adversaries being the variables in different scenarios. As the noted inventor and entrepreneur Joe Altieri says, 'A towering truth about leadership: It is the little things. Those "little things" are what will help to build trust and respect in your leadership and endear you to your staff.' To put it most simplistically as a very famous quote goes, 'Leadership is not one big thing; it is a million little things.' What are these little things? Just to count a few of them, leaders inspire, motivate, find solutions for complex challenges, set benchmarks and achievable targets, stay ahead of their adversaries/competitors, work towards achieving organizational goals, foster team spirit by valuing the contribution of each member of the team, build trust, manage crises and keep the passion alive among their team members. In addition, leaders ensure individual and collective discipline, understand their own DNA, the team's DNA and the organization's DNA to optimize their convergences while minimizing the divergences.

Leaders Take Ownership

Leaders create a happy team and a happy workplace by synergizing the collective energies of their team members for the optimal utilization of the existing resources to achieve the team's objectives. Leaders take ownership of the task at hand and make every member of the team an equal stakeholder in it. Leaders also spend time on planning for the future, devising strategies for the growth of each member in the organization, based on the prevalent opportunities and contingencies. It is this attribute of enthusiastically striving for collective excellence and growth through synergized action that distinguishes a good leader from a pedantic short-sighted manager obsessed with personal development. In this way, a leader truly personifies Abraham Lincoln's definition of success as 'going from failure to failure without loss of enthusiasm'. This aspect is discussed in detail in a later chapter.

Leaders Enable

An important quality of a good leader is facilitation, as an efficient leader enables people to give their best by laying out the road map for them to achieve their vision and goals. To ensure this enabling atmosphere, leaders create a work ethos with imaginative processes, structures and systems for people to succeed in the face of all odds and challenges. Taking it further, leaders create a work ethos, working culture and a propitious operating environment for people to produce their best under the given circumstances, whereas managers and CEOs direct people with the sole aim of attaining set targets with utter disregard to simmering resistance or a stressful working environment. It would be no exaggeration to say that leaders impact their teams and organizations through their sheer presence, quietly resolving problems without making much ado about their contributions. This trait is appositely summed up by the award-winning comedian and television host Jimmy Carr, who points out, 'Everyone is jealous of what you got but no one is jealous of how you got it.' In the army too, it is the medal or the trophy won by a soldier that grabs all the

attention, not the rigorous training, hard work and their ability to stake even their life for the accomplishment of the mission that enable him to attain the prize. It sums up the way successful people are judged at the surface not knowing what lies beneath.

Leaders Work with a Purpose

Irrespective of whether a leader is born, trained or honed by situations in life, one personality trait that a leader must always possess is to be keenly aware of the purpose of his actions and what his ultimate aim in life is. This situation is defined as working for the 'end state' in the army. I am reminded of the parable of a Mexican fisherman and an American traveller that I read many years ago. This story could function as a guiding light for any leader, enabling them to assess the situation calmly, re-analyse, reallocate targets and roles and pragmatically lay down the goals for the team. Here is a brief excerpt from the parable:[2]

The Parable of the Mexican Fisherman

An American investment banker was at the pier of a small coastal Mexican village when a small boat with just one fisherman docked. Inside the small boat were several large yellowfin tuna. The American complimented the Mexican on the quality of his fish and asked how long it took to catch them.

The Mexican replied, 'Only a little while.'

The American then asked why didn't he stay out longer and catch more fish.

The Mexican said he had enough to support his family's immediate needs.

The American then asked, 'But what do you do with the rest of your time?'

---

[2] Source: https://aliabdaal.com/newsletter/the-parable-of-the-mexican-fisherman/.

The Mexican fisherman said, 'I sleep late, fish a little, play with my children, take siestas with my wife, Maria, and stroll into the village each evening where I sip wine, and play guitar with my amigos. I have a full and busy life.'

The American scoffed. 'I have an MBA from Harvard, and can help you,' he said. 'You should spend more time fishing, and with the proceeds, buy a bigger boat. With the proceeds from the bigger boat, you could buy several boats, and eventually you would have a fleet of fishing boats. Instead of selling your catch to a middle-man, you could sell directly to the processor, eventually opening up your own cannery. You could control the product, processing, and distribution,' he said. 'Of course, you would need to leave this small coastal fishing village and move to Mexico City, then Los Angeles, and eventually to New York City, where you will run your expanding enterprise.'

The Mexican fisherman asked, 'But, how long will all this take?'

To which the American replied, 'Oh, fifteen to twenty years or so.'

'But what then?' asked the Mexican.

The American laughed and said, 'That's the best part. When the time is right, you would announce an IPO, and sell your company stock to the public and become very rich. You would make millions!'

'Millions – then what?'

The American said, 'Then you could retire. Move to a small coastal fishing village where you could sleep late, fish a little, play with your kids, take siestas with your wife and stroll to the village in the evenings where you could sip wine and play guitar with your amigos.'

The irony of this parable should not be lost on a real leader who works with the end state in mind.

Leaders Insist, Persist and Prevail

Some glowing examples of individuals without acclaimed parentage or formal training emerging as successful leaders pertain to the great generous and kind warrior Danveer Karna and Eklavya from the epic Mahabharata. Danveer Karna was disowned by his own mother and brothers, yet he became an exceptionally courageous and conscientious warrior. Eklavya, on the other hand, was a young hunter prince with aspirations of becoming a skilled archer, who sought training from the renowned scholar and warrior, Guru Dronacharya, also an archery coach to the royal Kuru family. When Dronacharya refused to train Eklavya on the grounds that he was not of blue blood, Eklavya created a clay statue of Dronacharya and meticulously practised archery in front of it. He eventually attained expertise in the craft that even exceeded the skills of Dronacharya's royal disciples. When Dronacharya learnt of Eklavya's mastery in the art, he demanded Eklavya's right thumb as a token of respect, to prevent Eklavya from becoming a better archer than his favourite disciple Arjun. In complete deference to the wishes of his guru, Eklavya immediately chopped off his thumb and presented it to Dronacharya. Leaders with unparalleled determination to succeed at all costs thus emerge as perpetual winners in the face of any odds. These examples amplify the subtle difference between 'I can win' and 'I will not lose'. 'I can win' is a desire to win, whereas 'I will not lose' is a determination to win.

Leaders Nurture a Winning Mindset

The media and public discourse often describe certain individuals, especially organizational heads or victorious electoral candidates, as winners. What distinguishes these people from the also-rans? How can we separate the grain from the chaff while choosing potential leaders? Do these leaders embody an 'X' factor or any unique attribute that goes beyond mere hard work and individual capabilities? My extensive experience in the military suggests that effective leaders may not always end up as winners by themselves but their positive and strong **winning mindset** acts as a motivating factor, inspiring the team or organization they are leading to nurture a winning work culture. This winning mindset of a leader over a period becomes the DNA of the organization which, in turn, produces winners from within the establishment. The credit can go to the leader but the most important thing to notice here is that the leader's winning mindset has imbued the team with a winning work culture and this produces many more winners in that organization.

Leaders Experiment

Leaders never shy away from shouldering responsibilities or going the extra mile to deliver results. This leadership trait is best summed up in the famous Jewish proverb, 'I ask not for a lighter burden, but for broader shoulders.' Another idiom that aptly defines a leader is 'Growth happens outside your comfort zone.' A comfort zone simply means a physical or a psychological state or working environment that causes lesser turbulence and lower levels of uncertainty and trepidation. People who prefer to stay confined in their comfort zones and avoid risk-taking tend to stagnate, often even accepting failure or drudgery rather than striving for success. A leader thus actively seeks discomfort, traversing journeys over and above the beaten path to achieve a higher purpose. Success is not a comfort zone thing; it's the result of

a very uncomfortable grind but a very sweet thing in the end when you are at the podium. So, **being uncomfortable to be comfortable** is the mantra. There is an ancient wisdom in knowing that no one ever achieved anything great by treading only a beaten path.

Risk-taking, Risk Aversion, Risk Absorption and Confidence

As mentioned above, **risk-taking** ability is one of the most critical aspects of decision-making. In my opinion, a decision merely based on culling all the available information and data, coupled with a cost-benefit analysis, would be an ordinary decision if devoid of the element of risk that would enable optimization of opportunities and gains. However, calculated risk-taking should not be confused with brash or whimsical behaviour leading to erratic or immature decisions. In contrast to risk-taking, **risk aversion** is a negative leadership trait that minimizes the scope of growth or opportunities for a leader. Another crucial characteristic of a leader is **risk absorption**, minutely discussed in both military war rooms and corporate boardrooms, signifying an assessment of the positive and negative impacts of all possible options and eventualities. This single-most formidable ability of a leader can convert an ordinary decision into a winning one. Risk absorption also has to be supported by extensive situational analysis and the gumption to face any adverse outcome of one's decision. Juxtaposed against risk-taking is the attribute of **confidence**, which may be defined as 'the feeling or belief that one can have faith in or rely on someone or something'. Confidence in one's own or one's team's capabilities may reflect the ability to handle difficult situations but **a leader must always shun overconfidence or a sense of complacency**, which usually spells disaster in the long term.

In the NDA, all cadets are required to write a dissertation and the topic of my dissertation was the 'Six-Day Arab–Israel War'. Just to refresh the reader's memory, Israel's triumph in the Six-Day Arab–Israel War in 1967 was so overwhelming that it imbued the young two-decade-old Jewish State with a sense of formidable and inviolable security despite being surrounded by hostile neighbours on all sides. As would have been expected in view of the dynamics of the volatile region, Israel's complacency was severely shaken during the Yom Kippur War of 1973, when it was completely taken by surprise by the Arab offensive launched on Yom Kippur, the holiest day of the year for Judaism. Yom Kippur, signifying the last Ten Days of Repentance, occurs annually on the tenth of Tishrei, corresponding to a date in late September or early October. The enormous impact of such an unexpected event on a nation is documented in the article 'The Hidden Calculation Behind the Yom Kippur War' by Michael Doran, written on 2 October 2023 in www.hudson.org. Here is an excerpt from the article:

> In his memoir, Ariel Sharon, the future Prime Minister of Israel who commanded a tank division in the Yom Kippur War, describes the confusion he witnessed among Israeli soldiers as they retreated in the face of overwhelming Egyptian firepower. 'I . . . saw something strange on their faces—not fear but bewilderment,' Sharon writes. 'Suddenly something was happening to them that had never happened before. These were soldiers who had been brought up on victories—not easy victories maybe, but nevertheless victories. Now they were in a state of shock. How could it be that these Egyptians were crossing the canal right in our faces?

How was it that they were moving forward, and we were defeated?'

When Israel's soldiers brought home their stories, the entire nation began debating this question—and has not stopped to this day. How did the vaunted Israeli intelligence agencies fail to see the war coming? Whose fault was it? What should have been done differently? Even the best answers to these questions tend to provide only an incomplete picture of the truth, and they sometimes frame the debate in misleading terms, focusing on the failure to anticipate the surprise attack while missing the larger military and diplomatic context.

This essay seeks to resolve a few of these arguments. It will show that even if Israeli leaders had known the attack was coming, they still would have underestimated its force. And their actions might not have been very different under any circumstance, rooted as they were in decisions made three years earlier.'[3]

And we all know what occurred on 7 October 2023, fifty years after the Yom Kippur War of 1973. Ironically, just five days after the publication of Doran's essay, and twelve days after Yom Kippur on 25 September 2023, Israel was yet again surprised by Hamas and several other terrorist groups. The breaching of Israeli defence lines and armed incursions into the Gaza Envelope of Southern Israel from the Gaza Strip was arguably the first invasion of Israeli territory since the 1948 Arab–Israeli War. In this surprise attack, many Israeli civilian men, women and children were killed, injured, raped

---

[3] Source: https://www.hudson.org/foreign-policy/hidden-calculation-behind-yom-kippur-war-michael-doran

and taken hostage by Hamas. It may be argued that this catastrophic event could perhaps have been avoided if Israel's political leadership and defence forces had not become complacent about their security needs over the years when relative peace reigned in the region.

Leaders Delegate

Leaders also believe in the power of delegation. Recognizing that every organization functions through the individual contributions of professionals in different domains, leaders appropriately delegate work to the people within the organization, concentrating on the big picture themselves. As you grow in hierarchy and job profile, delegating allows you time and space to handle more critical or important assignments as also provides opportunities for grooming and mentoring subordinates to take up the greater challenges with enhanced capabilities in future. This delegation is what allows 'seniors' to subtly graduate to becoming 'mentors' for their junior staff.

Are Leaders Born or Can They Be Trained?

Leaders Emerge from Real-Life Situations

The question asked most often in all leadership and management debates is, 'Are leaders born or can they be trained?' But no answer has ever been a 'one-size-fits-all' reply. If leaders were born, then the offspring or siblings of every leader who was successful or admired should be born leaders too. However, the charisma and leadership traits of many great military leaders, political stalwarts, social activists and even business tycoons do not run in the family. To bring in my personal experience here, I have been part of some of the toughest military training regimes during my service life. Such training is meant to impart the toughest attack and survival skills to all kinds of military

commanders, ranging from a section commander in charge of a team of ten men to a higher commander commanding a brigade or higher formations. The training courses are also named accordingly, for example, a section commander's course, platoon commander's course, junior command course, senior command course or higher command course. Interestingly, none of these courses is called a leader's course. The subtle difference between a commander and a leader lies in the fact that while military commanders are appointed on the basis of their experience, service and suitability to command a particular formation or a body of troops in a particular operational environment, military leaders emerge from real-life situations, be they related to active combat or otherwise.

Leaders Have No Age Bar

For selection as an officer in the defence forces, an aspirant has to clear a written entrance examination, followed by evaluation by the Services Selection Board (SSB) and a medical fitness test before being called to join a pre-commissioning training academy. The three steps for clearing the SSB assessment include psychological evaluation, Group Testing Officer (GTO) tasks and an interview. The GTO tasks include various indoor and outdoor activities comprising, amongst other assessment techniques, group discussions, group planning exercises, collective group tasks, individual obstacle crossings and command tasks—all aimed at gauging a candidate's communication skills, planning abilities, team spirit, physical stamina, mental toughness, leadership traits and maturity in handling key responsibilities. During this exercise, lasting over a few weeks, the defence aspirants are assessed 24/7 on the above-mentioned qualities by a panel of experts and experienced professionals. No minimum or

maximum quantifiable standards need to be achieved during the GTO tasks, nor do the given problems have any templates as answers. Interestingly, the candidates, both male and female, and often as young as sixteen years or so, at times suggest unorthodox but pragmatic solutions to some highly complex tasks, thereby defying the belief that leaders mature with age. Many of the youngsters have exhibited their leadership mantle beyond their age while performing the GTO tasks mandated by the SSB, which has thus emerged as a scientific method for selecting future leaders from the available talent pool.

Leaders Emerge from the Teams

As discussed earlier, leaders do emerge from the situations that confront them. All of us, as part of a team, at some stage in our lives, have come across situations where we could have made a difference but chose to ignore it and go on our way because that situation did not affect the team directly or we did not want to get involved in someone else's issues. Opportunity knocks on everyone's door; it depends on how one responds to it. That response dictates whether one will emerge as a leader or remain content with being led as a member of the team. This brings us to the aspect that leaders are neither born nor trained but they emerge from within the teams and situations—the more difficult the situation, the more effective the solution and more successful the leader. Of course, these leadership qualities are continuously honed through structured and non-structured training to make them effective commanders of the future. With the passage of time, some of these young men and women emerge as effective leaders while commanding the troops under their command in different combat situations. The important aspect to be understood from the GTO tasks evaluation system is

that being a dependable team player always helps as **leaders emerge from the teams** while facing difficult situations.

How to Identify a Leader

Leaders Care

A good leader will always appear to be a calm person on the surface even if a tempest is raging within them. Successful leaders carry much more than talent within them, adroitly commanding men and women, and managing human resources, deeply impacting people's lives through their actions. Adherence to morals, compassion and commiseration with people's sensitivities are some of the less publicized traits of a leader, as it is these soft qualities that help build successful armies or businesses. Here, it would be appropriate to broadly cite the inspirational speaker and author Simon Sinek, who suggests that 'Leadership is not about being in charge. It's about taking care of those in your charge. Great leaders are like great parents. They're always learning AND make sure those in their care benefit from what they've learned.'

Leaders Own Their Mistakes

The best of leaders can have a bad day in office when they make a 'not-so-good' decision, which naysayers may call a 'mistake' with the wisdom of hindsight. However, instead of being demoralized by this setback, leaders should be able to own their mistakes, and be willing to learn from them as they are the best teachers in life. A gloomy yesterday is bound to be followed by a beautiful today and a promising tomorrow. The manner in which leaders handle mistakes reflects their inner strength and values. Further, a leader who displays a good sense of humour even in the most challenging situations

passes the litmus test of leadership. Subtle humour can liven up any war room or a boardroom in such situations, chiefly when it comes from the leader.

Leaders Take It on the Chin

A military or corporate leader needs to show real grit and determination particularly when the journey is tough and the road is dotted with obstacles. Students in all high-altitude training schools and institutions are taught how to escape snowstorms in the mountains. Even animals exhibit the same instinct to run when they perceive danger, barring the bison, which is the only animal that stands up to face a snowstorm instead of running away from impending death. Thus, bison-like, a leader should know how to face arduous and burdensome situations head-on and combat them before they assume mammoth proportions and become more menacing.

Leaders Know the Art of Self-Management

The oft-discussed concept of time management, though significant in itself, is just one constituent of 'self-management'. Former CEO of Apple Steve Jobs asserted, 'The greatest people are self-managing. They don't need to be managed. Once they know what to do, they'll go figure out how to do it.' Similarly, when the renowned English footballer and sports broadcaster Gary Lineker, OBE (Order of the British Empire), was asked, 'Who scores the most number of goals? Is he the person who is at the right place at the right time?', he replied, 'No, you have to be at the right place all the time, then sometimes the ball comes to you.' This statement is a classic example of how to manage yourself all the time. A leader, too, has to constantly be 'at the right place all the time' to influence the outcomes of any situation.

Leaders Make Their Presence Felt

An individual's personality is also a reflection of character, with attire being an intrinsic part of this persona. In this context, the concept of 'power dressing', which does not necessarily have to do with expensive clothes or branded accessories, is a function of body language or the sheer presence and charisma of the individual. Thus, even if dressed in dungarees while supervising operations on the production floor of a factory or in combat uniform in a military field area, the way in which leaders carry themselves, irrespective of their outfit, is what denotes their power and position. Most of us would be aware of the incident pertaining to Group Captain Abhinandan Varthaman, Vir Chakra, the daredevil Indian Air Force fighter pilot whose MiG-21 Bison plane scrambled from the Srinagar Air Force base to intercept state-of-the-art US-made F-16 planes flown by the Pakistan Air Force over Indian territory on 27 February 2019. Although he shot down an enemy plane in a fierce mid-air dogfight, his MiG-21 was targeted and he was taken into custody by Pakistani forces. However, facing the relentless pressure of Indian diplomacy and the threat of its military retaliation, Pakistan released Abhinandan at the Attari border outpost near Amritsar on the night of 1 March 2019. When he walked back across the Indian border shorn of his Air Force uniform and dressed in an ill-fitting suit, probably procured from the local market in Lahore at short notice by his Pakistani captors, what struck people the most was Group Captain Abhinandan's graceful demeanour, dignified body language, alert visage despite an eye injury and warrior's walk with his head held high. This was a perfect example of power dressing by a leader and a soldier who had displayed unparalleled heroics in the battlefield and that swag was not lost even during his subsequent captivity by the enemy.

Leaders Are Witty Teachers

I recall another incident during my tenure as a young lieutenant in Udaipur, Rajasthan, in 1985–86. Lieutenant General Nathu Singh Rathore, a highly respected Indian Army veteran from the erstwhile princely state of Dungarpur, came to stay in the guest room of our officers' mess during his visit to Udaipur. He was the second Indian officer to have graduated from Sandhurst, UK, before Independence. Soon after Independence, he was offered the post of commander-in-chief of the Indian Army to replace the retiring British officer General Roy Bucher, in 1949. Showcasing the highest traditions of the Indian Army, Lieutenant General Rathore declined this offer, stating that General K.M. Cariappa, who was senior to him, was more eligible for the post. That evening, as he was enjoying the breeze from Lake Pichola, and the view of the royal Lake Palace and simmering lights of Jag Mandir in the middle of the lake, I joined him with a drink to revel in his military experiences and anecdotes. As I saw the depleted drink in his glass, I rose and politely offered, 'Sir, can I get you another drink?' Immediately, the general quipped, 'Young man, by offering *another drink*, you are trying to remind your guest that he has already had one drink. You never mention "another drink". Instead you should simply ask, "Sir, can I get you a drink?"' I stood both humbled and enlightened by this great lesson in *mehman-nawazi* (hospitality) and mannerisms imparted in such a suave and subtle manner. Disclaimer: Here, it is in no way suggested that the consumption of alcohol is encouraged or advocated in any manner; yet the anecdote is featured to

highlight the subtleness of the mode of conveying a point by an effective leader, even during a social interaction.

Leaders Choose to Do the Right Things

Choosing the 'harder right' instead of the 'easier wrong' is one principle that always guided me in my professional life, with some great results. This value is instilled in an NDA cadet from the very beginning as the cadet commences his rigorously disciplined training and goes through the routine of reciting the NDA prayer every morning throughout the three years of his training. I can faultlessly recite the same prayer even today after the passage of so many decades since I passed out of the NDA. Even more importantly, I still derive the same strength and motivation from this prayer that I did as a seventeen-year-old cadet donning the khaki uniform for the first time. I recite this prayer here with the same respect and awe that it evoked in me each time I said it all those years ago:

O God, help us to keep ourselves physically strong, mentally awake and morally straight, that in doing our duty to Thee and our country we may keep the honour of the Services untarnished.

Strengthen us to guard our country from external aggression and internal disorders.

*Awaken our admiration for honest dealing and clean thinking, and guide us to **choose the harder right instead of the easier wrong**.*

Kindle our hearts with fellowship for our comrades at arms and with loyalty to the men we command.

Endow us with the courage which is born of the love of what is noble and which knows no compromise or retreat when truth and right are in peril.

Grant us new opportunities of service to Thee, to our country and to the men we lead, and ever help us to place such service before self.

A Leader Motivates the Team to Achieve Victory

The motto of my regiment, the Rajputana Rifles, *Veer Bhogya Vasundhara*, means 'The brave shall inherit the earth' in Sanskrit. My life and service have played out by living by this motto every single day of my existence since I joined the regiment. This motto is not merely a spiritual evocation or a military mantra but actually a soldier's resolve to win by adopting a 'do-or-die' strategy. As Lord Krishna advised Arjun at the helm of the latter's chariot in the Kurukshetra battle of the Mahabharata, 'When you fight, you will either be slain on the battlefield and go to the celestial abodes, or you will gain victory and enjoy the kingdom on earth.' Similarly, leaders inspire men and women to fight for the righteous cause and strive for victory, irrespective of others' opinions about the warrior or his mission. This is lucidly recounted by the Hindi poet Sandeep Dwivedi, in his couplet:

जिसको रखनी धार है, उसे तो घिसना पड़ेगा ।
बहुत कुछ सुनना पड़ेगा, बहुत कुछ सहना पड़ेगा ॥

(He who wants to maintain a sharp edge has to go through the grind. He has to listen to many a thing and bear many a thing.)

'Life is all about a card game. Choosing the right cards is not in our hands. But playing well with the cards in hand determines our success.'

—Bal Gangadhar Tilak

4

Leaders Constitute Winning Teams

आत्मज्ञानं समारम्भः तितिक्षा धर्मनित्यता ।
यमर्थान्नापकर्षन्ति स वै राजर्षिः उच्यते ॥

(They who are not overwhelmed by the challenges of
life owing to their knowledge, persistence, patience and
virtue are the wise, deserving a position of leadership.)

How Does a Leader Build Chemistry with the Team?

Is a Leader as Good as the Team They Lead?

There can be differing opinions about the manner in which
a leader connects with the team, but one constant is
that leaders are an integral part of the team, neither above nor
beyond it.

In fact, leaders who refrain from using a hands-on
approach and remain insulated from their teams usually end
up creating a 'he/she' versus 'we' syndrome within the team,
resulting in avoidable friction and communication gaps. Such
a Gordian knot can be adroitly avoided through building
intuitive leader-team dynamics, pragmatic decision-making
and carrying together all members of the team with diverse
personalities, wherein everyone is made to feel like a winner.

The relationship between the team and its leader is akin to that between a car and its driver. The two complement each other, as for driving the car efficiently, the driver needs to be skilful, and the car, too, needs to be in a perfect roadworthy condition to enable the driver to run it skilfully. Here, it may be argued that this commensal relationship would be rendered redundant by the advent of driverless cars or robo-taxis that can operate with minimal or no human interface. However, self-driven cars can also operate effectively only under the most favourable or ideal driving conditions. They could run into trouble when confronted with challenges, such as inclement weather, foggy conditions and violation of traffic rules by other vehicles plying on the road. The analogy can be taken further for both the war room and the boardroom, as neither military combat situations nor business dealings can be as predictable or reliable as a robotic car steered by a non-human controller. Hence, it is imperative to assign an experienced leader to a team in such situations. The most critical aspect of a model showcasing a successful team and leader can be encapsulated as follows: The concept of 'What a leader is, what a leader knows and what a leader does' must be collaboratively synergized with the energies and expertise of individual team members, enabling them to contribute to a shared vision.

A Team is More Than the Sum of Its Parts

A team is much more than merely a group of people working together in the same organization at the same time. It is an amalgam of professionals who may be individually competent but should be able to perform flawlessly collectively to accomplish a common mission. For achieving this perfect synergy, it is crucial to acknowledge and appreciate the role of

each and every member of the team in their shared task, and this is where a compassionate leader steps in, rising above the clinical role of a manager. If the team were a troupe of artists, a manager may appreciate the play only if the show is houseful, but a leader will celebrate them for their performance and not the number of people in the audience. Such a leader intuitively realizes the value of boosting the morale of each team member to shape them into assets rather than berating any of them for a below-par performance, which could turn them instead into non-productive liabilities for the team. If a team member is not appreciated for their efforts and is always taunted about their results or lack of them, it is the surest way of turning a willing contributor into an irritated, non-communicative, non-cooperative and non-productive worker, just available at the place of work. In sum and substance, they turn from being a long-term asset to an immediate liability. Irrespective of what your position is in the organization, one golden rule is: **'When dealing with people, be a leader, not a manager.'**

Team Spirit
Linking this to the concept of team spirit in the army, it is not without reason that collective participation in sports is considered the most preferred activity for cementing the bond among soldiers and for enhancing team spirit. Indeed, a sports field is believed to be the ideal breeding ground for future leaders. It would be pertinent to recall the oft-cited war quotation, 'The Battle of Waterloo was won on the playing fields of Eton', attributed to Arthur Wellesley (1769–1852), the first Duke of Wellington and a graduate of Eton College in England. Wellesley was alluding to the highly acclaimed British school, Eton, where young men were rigorously trained for a career in the military, and sports were considered crucial for

inculcating the virtues of team spirit, discipline and planning in the boys at an early age. Significantly, Wellesley, along with Marshal Blücher, led the coalition of British and allied armies at Waterloo against the powerful French commander Napoleon Bonaparte, humbling the latter in the battlefield and putting an end to the French aspiration for domination of Europe.

Honour Code: Honour, A Sacrosanct Code

'My Buddy Is My God, He Will Save My Life'

Most people tend to believe that the Indian Army is explicitly governed by the Army Act and Army Rules. While this belief is correct in letter, it goes way beyond it in spirit. I would like to reiterate without any doubt that the soldiers and officers of the Indian Army live and die by the 'Honour Code', described as follows: *The Honour Code is a sacrosanct code or a set of rules or ideals that define what is considered honourable behaviour within a community. It's based on the idea that people can be trusted to act honourably, and [it] can be imposed by individuals, cultures, societies, or institutions.*

Various institutions follow their own written or unwritten codes of honour. For instance, the honour code of the Indian Institute of Technology (IIT) Gandhinagar is defined as a set of values that students are expected to follow, premised on the idea that people will do the right thing under all circumstances. In another educational institution, the Western Sydney University, the student honour code has interestingly been developed by the students themselves, laying down guidelines for them to act with academic integrity in all situations.

In the Indian military, the most commendable and ethical code for a soldier is, **'The Indian Army does not leave anyone behind, not even our dead.'** The most

conspicuous aspects of this code are camaraderie and esprit de corps. Recently, in a conversation with one of my dear friends, Major General Anil Chaudhary, Sena Medal (Retd), a daredevil officer and an excellent sportsman in the NDA, he narrated an incident pertaining to the Kargil War of 1999, assigning it the title 'My leader would have carried me along'. He recalled that he was commanding an infantry brigade in Ladakh sector in 2010. This particular brigade had actively participated in the Kargil War in 1999. As a brigadier in 2010, while supervising the preparation of defences in the forward area during an annual training exercise, he met a serving NCO on leave at his village near the Line of Control (LoC), who had served in the Ladakh Scouts during the Kargil War. The discussion revealed that the NCO had been decorated with the Sena Medal (Gallantry) award for his brave act during the Kargil War. During the period May–June 1999, amidst reports of the presence of militants (who later turned out to be Pakistani soldiers) in the forward high-altitude areas of Northern Ladakh sectors, many patrols were launched all along the front to assess the ground situation. A small team of the XYZ Wing (now Ladakh Scouts), of which this NCO (a young soldier during the war) was a member, was launched in a particular area along the LoC. As this team, composed of troops from Ladakh who are the sons of the soil, led by a JCO, reached close to a peak, they came under heavy enemy fire. The fire, directed downwards from a vantage point, hit all the team members but this young soldier was spared. Subsequently, he too was hit by a bullet in the leg and to avoid any further damage, he did not move, feigning death. Meanwhile, reacting to the SOS message from the patrol leader, the Indian Artillery had moved in and started shelling the suspected location of the enemy, forcing them to run back to their bunkers.

In the increasing darkness, with his patrol leader JCO lying dead next to him, the young soldier, who too was severely injured with a bullet in his thigh, decided that it was time for courageous action. With no food or water, and no means of communicating with headquarters, he weighed his options and commenced his descent from the peak, dragging the dead body of his leader, who was incidentally much heavier than him. He crawled for almost three days, surviving only on water extracted by crushing the available snow in the valley but finally made it to the location of his unit along with the mortal remains of his leader. Moved by the narration of his actions, when Major General Chaudhary asked him, 'Why did you carry the dead body of your leader?', his nonchalant answer was, '**I had full faith in my leader and my team, that in case something like this had happened to me, I too would never be left behind. So, how could I leave my leader behind?**' He further said, '*Saab, JCO saab ko upar hi chhodkar main paltan mein wapis kaise jata?* (Sir, leaving the JCO there, how could I return to the battalion?).' This tale of exceptional endurance and commitment by an Indian soldier brought tears to my eyes but also made my heart swell with pride. Although this soldier could not save the life of his buddy/leader in this case, his extraordinary action reflects the highest traditions of the Indian Army and its honour code. This kind of commitment and living by the code of honour must also be imbibed by young entrepreneurs and corporate leaders. While these codes may differ in letter across business houses, their underlying spirit must always remain the same.

My Flag Is My Honour

As discussed in an earlier chapter, the words '*Naam, Namak, Nishan*' are engraved in the heart of every Indian soldier. Saving the honour of 'my flag' is not only a solemn duty for a soldier but actually a ritual embedded in their very being, making them salute the national flag every time they see it. They stand guard on the flag under the sun, snow, rain and winds to protect its honour and pride. And when the situation arises, they face enemy bullets head-on and lay down their life protecting the honour of the motherland, earning the ultimate honour of coming back home wrapped in the national flag. In the olden days when the regimental nishan was carried on to the battlefield, there were many heroic tales of soldiers laying down their lives trying to save the nishan, even preventing it from falling to the ground during any assault.

One of the salient features of the code for India's flag is that it represents the hopes and aspirations of the people of India. As a symbol of our national pride, it evokes universal affection, respect and loyalty, occupying a special place in our collective psyche. This emotion is echoed in the words of Elmer Davis, a Peabody Award-winning American news reporter and director of the United States Office of War Information during World War II, 'This nation (referring to the United States) will remain the land of the free only so long as it is the home of the brave.' Carrying this principle into the corporate world, profit-making can be concurrently achieved while safeguarding the national interest as a non-negotiable element of business strategy, as exhibited by our armed forces. The Tata Group is one corporate house in India that follows such a code of ethics in its business model while keeping the 'nation first' as a code of honour; an organization that has achieved financial success and public respect in equal measure.

Respect the Dead Enemy

Another code of honour for the Indian Army is to accord respect to the dead soldiers of the enemy. It is a soldier's inviolable duty to resolutely fight for his nation and neutralize the enemy during any war. However, once the enemy soldier has died fighting on the battlefield, the code of honour for the Indian soldier changes to respecting the mortal remains of the enemy soldiers who died an honourable death fighting for their country. This honour code has always been meticulously followed by Indian soldiers. Recall here the 1971 Bangladesh War, wherein the Indian Army not only saved 93,000 Pakistani prisoners of war (POWs) from an irate Bangla mob but also housed them in various camps, offering them the same treatment as meted out to guests in an Indian home, adhering to the culture of '*Atithi Devo Bhava*', which translates as 'A Guest Is Like God'.

Another recent example of this code is from the Kargil War, when the Pakistani troops and government refused to accept the mortal remains of their dead soldiers, even when offered by the Indian side. Ultimately, it was the Indian Army that gave them a decent burial as per their religious rituals. The Pakistan Army, on the other hand, not only killed the Indian soldiers whom they had captured alive but also mutilated their dead bodies in a dastardly manner, chopping off their limbs and gouging out their eyeballs. This incident highlights the glaring difference between an ethical army and an immoral army.

'*Nischay Kar Apni Jeet Karo*'

'*Nischay kar apni jeet karo* (My determination will make me triumphant)', the motto of the Sikh Regiment of the Indian Army, has been taken from one of the most celebrated and widely quoted hymns of the tenth Sikh Guru, Sri Guru Gobind Singhji. The complete hymn is as follows:

'Deh Siva bar mohe eha, subh karman te kabhu na taro.
Na daro arr seo jab jaye laro, nischey kar apni jit karo.
Arr Sikh ho apne he mann ko, eh laalach hou gun
tau ucharo.
Jab aav ki audh nidan bane att he rann me tabh joojh maro.

This translates as 'Dear God, grant my request so that I may never deviate from doing good deeds. That, I shall have no fear of the enemy when I go into battle and with determination I will be victorious. That, I may teach my mind to only sing your praises, and when the time comes, I should die fighting heroically on the field of battle.'

Following this honour code of *'Nischay kar apni jeet karo'*, my unit, the Fourth Battalion of the Rajputana Rifles (4 RAJRIF), has earned 210 individual awards post-Independence, and 346 in the pre-Independence era. On seven occasions, during more than 204 years of its existence, the unit has suffered over 200 casualties in a single operation and still hit back with renewed resolve and emerged victorious.

This winning ethos and never-say-die spirit embraced by every unit of the Indian Army could also be imbibed by corporate entities, enabling them to overcome competition and achieve their organizational goals while combating challenges during their journeys. A true leader realizes the importance of such a commitment and the mandate to follow the principle of *'Nischay kar apni jeet karo'*, to create a winning culture among their team.

The Inviolability of Trust

No Leader Can Achieve Success Single-Handedly

The renowned Indian actor Anupam Kher once recounted in an interview that during his days of struggle in the film industry, he

never spent time with other struggling actors as the latter would only discuss stories of their failures, which generated a lot of negativity. Instead of spending time with his counterparts, Kher would prefer to meditate in a temple to renew his energies and imbibe positivity in his effort. Similarly, in the army too, numerous adventure and sports activities are organized for soldiers to enable them to overcome their worries, adopt a positive attitude and focus on winning the game or conquering the challenge posed to them. Since in all such team activities, the entire team works together with a positive mindset, it is important to include inspiring people in the team who optimize their capabilities for achieving the goals laid out before them.

In maritime parlance, team effort is like a sailboat wherein every member of the crew ostensibly pulls the strings of the sails in different directions but the boat moves in a focused manner in a single designated direction. It is this inherent shared trust that all members will individually contribute their best to foster team spirit for attaining the objective. It can also be like a canoe race where every member of the crew is paddling in unison and the boat moves in the desired direction. In both cases, the direction in which the individuals are pulling or pushing is not relevant—it is the trust of each team member that the others are doing their part in the best interest of the team that matters. What appears may not always be true, hence being non-judgemental helps in building trust and team spirit. Another example of trust in a team is the way volleyball players shift and occupy another player's position when that player has dived off the court for a difficult pick.

Leaders Inspire Faith and Bravery
In the Services Selection Board, most of the aspirants are rejected for exhibiting negative qualities. This selection

criterion is based on the premise that existing positive attributes are easy to hone in a candidate and can also be inculcated during training if they are absent, but it is difficult to extirpate negative traits. Similarly, in the corporate world, it is advisable to filter out people with any negative habits during the selection of a team. The significance of acquiring and building a positive attitude has been evocatively etched in Charlie Mackesy's book, *The Boy, the Mole, the Fox and the Horse*, known for its famous quip from the protagonist boy, 'Sometimes I think you believe in me more than I do.' 'You'll catch up,' replied the horse.

I recall here my experience during the merciless Punjabi summer of 1976, when I was studying in the eleventh grade at Ferozepur. Accompanied by two of my classmates, Jagjit Singh Dhami and Haresh Jang Bahadur, I embarked on a cycle ride to Ferozeshah, a small village about 18 kilometres away from the district town of Ferozepur. The name Ferozeshah is etched in our national history, as it was here that a decisive battle was fought during the First Anglo-Sikh War (1845–46) between the British East India Company and the Sikh Empire, on 21–22 December 1845. Shah Mohammad (1780–1862), a Punjabi poet who lived during the reign of Maharaja Ranjit Singh (1780–1839), is best known for his book *Jangnama* (Book of War) written around 1846, which describes the First Anglo-Sikh War that took place after the death of Maharaja Ranjit Singh in 1839. Shah Mohammad had this to say about the bravery of the Sikh soldiers who fought fearlessly but were eventually vanquished in this war due to the absence of a leader of the calibre of Maharaja Ranjit Singh and treachery by their own during these wars. These lines are inscribed at the entrance of the Anglo-Sikh War Memorial at Ferozeshah:

Shah Mohammada Singhan Ne Gorian De
Wang Nimbuan Lahu Nichor Ditte
Je Kar Hondi Sarkar Taan Mul Paandee
Jehrian Khalse Ne Teghan Maarian Ne
Shah Mohamada Ik Sarkar Bajon
Faujan Jit Ke Annt Nuun Haarian Ne

Simply translated into English, this narration would read as, 'Sikh soldiers squeezed the British soldiers' blood, as one squeezes lemon. If Maharaja Ranjit Singh had been alive, he would have appreciated and honoured the Sikh soldiers for bravery the way Sikh soldiers fought valiantly with swords. But for the *Sarkar* (Maharaja Ranjit Singh), Sikhs having won, ultimately lost.'

Coming back to our bicycle journey to this revered place, Haresh, who was a proficient swimmer and a good boxer, decided to take a dip in the fast-flowing canal to beat the summer heat. Both Jagjit and I, being non-swimmers, advised Haresh against this dangerous adventure, but he refused to pay heed, jokingly even suggesting that he had faith that we would save him should things go wrong. Alarmingly, the current in the canal was so strong that Haresh was literally swept away by the water, drifting and drowning. Despite his boxing skills, Haresh could not fight the waves relentlessly coming towards him through the strong water current. Jagjit and I kept cycling along the canal track, trying to keep pace with our friend drifting in the canal. As our friend looked at us desperately for help, we remembered his words expressing faith that we would save him from trouble. Cycling ahead at a rapid pace, we removed our turbans and tied them together. Then, we threw the knotted end of the turbans in the canal enjoining Haresh to catch the flowing garment. Thankfully,

Haresh was able to catch hold of the turban's end and we managed to pull him out safely. As he thanked us profusely for our efforts after recovering from the misadventure, I can never forget what Jagjit told him, 'You had reposed faith in us, albeit jokingly, so how could we belie your trust, especially at the place where our forefathers fought for the honour of our land and the trust of our people.' Carrying forward this spirit, the three of us are still the best of friends even after almost half a century, with our next generations, too, carrying on with the tradition. This incident reinforces the belief that committed team members will always stand up for their teammates in every situation and never abuse the trust reposed in them by their colleagues and counterparts.

A Leader's Physical Presence Invokes Confidence in the Team

A leader's physical presence and involvement are critical for promoting confidence among the team, especially during uncertain or stressful situations or when the stakes are high. An example is that of the Badami Bagh Cantonment in Srinagar, which houses the Chinar Corps headquarters. Some of the families of the officers and soldiers deployed on the LoC or in counterterrorism operations areas within the Kashmir Valley also reside inside this garrison. Prior to 2019, cinema halls in the Valley had been lying locked for the preceding thirty-odd years. Hence, as a welfare measure for the soldiers and their families, the Chinar Corps used to screen the latest Hindi or regional language movies in the military movie hall inside the garrison called the Chinar Auditorium. This was intended to provide some sort of entertainment to the army community at a time of intense stress and violence during the year 2019, which was marked by the Pulwama improvised explosive device (IED) blast, the Balakot air strikes and the tension following the abrogation of Articles 370 and 35A in Jammu and Kashmir. In view of the heightened security during the period, the soldiers' family members residing inside the garrison were treated to movies in the Chinar Auditorium.

As the corps commander, I was well aware of the anxious moments experienced by the family members of the army personnel. Although I am not a great fan of Hindi movies, I would make it a point to watch each and every movie exhibited at the auditorium, and interact with the families and the children. Seeing the corps commander visibly relaxed and having a peaceful recreational evening served to reassure the families that all was well and that their husbands or fathers deployed in the forward areas were safe. I did not realize the full import of my gesture at the time but it was brought home to me much later when my wife and I met a soldier's wife at a *Barakhana* (community dinner) in Delhi, who highlighted the impact of my presence and calm demeanour in tough times. A visibly calm leader's presence can act as a reassurance for young team members. A light pat on the shoulder or a small thumbs-up can actually make the adrenaline levels shoot up amongst the team.

As discussed in an earlier chapter, delegation is the surest way to build confidence. As my seniority in the army hierarchy kept rising, whenever I delegated any task, I felt that I was achieving two objectives simultaneously. First, I was announcing to the team that I had trust in their capabilities, and second, as a leader, I was grooming the next generation of officers for the tactical and operational-level tasks that I had been performing myself till then. Delegation of duties allowed me more time to think and act at a strategic level

without getting bogged down with tactical and operational issues. Delegation is also an intrinsic part of the ecosystem of a hierarchical organization like the military, and is equally relevant in the corporate world, where the expansion of business necessitates the deployment of more hands and brains.

Managing Moods

Another relevant aspect of building confidence in the team is a leader's ability to manage moods. Recently, I received a message reflecting severe concern from a younger relative, a successful entrepreneur, who seemed to be facing distress and despondency. The chat message from the relative read, 'I am going to be 40 in the next three years and till date I have done nothing worthwhile in life.' I told the person that when I was at a similar age, I was fighting terrorists in the jungles of Lolab in North Kashmir as a major, without bothering if my life could be classified as 'worthwhile' or not. The real goal should be to not only gain experience offered by opportune circumstances but also to enjoy the experience while it lasts. Further, there is no age limit to restrain one from doing 'worthwhile' things. My personal experience is an apt reflection of this mantra. Having retired from the army at the age of sixty, I could well have sat back to enjoy my retired life. Instead, I decided to write a book immediately after retirement that became a national bestseller and won prestigious awards, constructed my house all by myself without appointing any architect, modelled for a motorcycle that I had always ridden passionately, both at age sixty-one, featured in a documentary and an ad film at the age of sixty-two, and am now writing my second book at age sixty-three. I have also been travelling extensively post retirement. So I would suggest to all who are interested in some practical advice, '**Don't count the years, but count your powers. Get up, tie your laces and run**.' The intention should be to generate happiness for others, and satisfaction for oneself for a deed well done, irrespective of one's age or occupation.

On another occasion, my wife Nita and I were on a road trip in a self-driven hired car during a vacation in Western Europe in 2012. Language was a barrier, especially because, with the swiftness with which we were moving from one country to another, certain words that we had picked up in one country were meaningless in the next one. Since Nita is very fond of tea and coffee, we were facing the challenge of not being able to explain that we wanted typical Indian household coffee (hand-beaten with sugar and water, and stirred in hot milk). Each time we halted at a roadside motel for coffee, we were offered something that was nowhere close to our own variant of coffee. This had a deleterious effect on Nita's mood, which was becoming increasingly irritable in the absence of the much-longed-for cup of her favourite drink. Finally, we halted at a café in Switzerland, which was literally in the middle of nowhere. After parking the car, I ventured out in an attempt to renew my quest for the evasive coffee.

The café was empty, and the middle-aged lady at the counter, who doubled up as a cook, couldn't understand a word of what I was saying, as I kept trying my luck by voicing words from all the European languages I had picked up during our trip over the last few weeks. Still unable to communicate with her, I tried sign language and thankfully it worked. I gestured to the lady asking if I could make my own coffee as there was no other customer in the café. She agreed, and I got down to the business of beating the sugar and coffee in a bowl and finally stirred it in a mug full of hot milk, all under the curious, watchful gaze of the café owner. On completion of my culinary adventure, I offered one mug to the lady at the counter, who sipped and gracefully nodded her appreciation. Then she said something I could partially understand that had something to do with me preparing that coffee. I carried the other cup of coffee to Nita who was still sitting in the car. Both thrilled and relieved at getting her favourite coffee, Nita said, 'Café owner *se iss* coffee *ka* local *naam aur* recipe *puchh kar aao* (Ask the owner the name and recipe of this coffee in the local language)', to which I replied, '*Woh* (café owner) *bhi iska naam aur* recipe *hi puchh rahi thi* (She was also asking me the name and recipe of this coffee).' Needless to say, the mood inside the car was much more amicable after this eventful coffee break, allowing us to more intuitively enjoy the beautiful Swiss countryside.

During another incident in 2013, as part of our National Defence College foreign tour, we (a group of fifteen brigadier and joint secretary-rank officers from the army, navy, air force, Indian Administrative Service [IAS], Indian Police Service [IPS] and some foreign officers with spouses) were travelling in a luxury coach through Zimbabwe. It was late in the afternoon when we drove off from Harare for Bulawayo, a distance of about 430 kilometres, which took seven-odd hours via bus. It was all going great and we were looking forward to a gala dinner being hosted for us by a non-resident Indian at his palatial residence in Bulawayo. However, it was getting dark and Bulawayo was still two hours away. Suddenly, in the middle of the thick African forest, the bus broke down. We all waited patiently while the local driver-cleaner duo tried to fix the problem. By now, it was pitch dark and getting suffocating inside the fixed windows bus without the air conditioner. The driver suggested that we should refrain from alighting from the bus in the middle of a jungle inhabited by wild animals like lions and elephants. Our military background soon gave a clear indication that the driver was a technical novice and would most likely fail in his attempt to repair the bus.

Meanwhile, a Gujarati colleague's wife took out her reserve stock of snacks, comprising fafda and methi puri, among other savouries. As the situation inside the bus was getting increasingly uneasy, I decided to take matters into my hands. Rising from my seat, I urged the cleaner to open the boot of the bus. Although initially reluctant, he eventually relented. Opening my suitcase, I pulled out the vodka bottles that I had picked up from the duty-free shop at the airport. All of a sudden, the party inside the bus warmed up, with more Gujarati snacks appearing, along with mineral water and soft drinks adding to the cocktails. Initially, only a few of us got down from the bus, standing close to the open bus doors to ensure an easy retreat inside the bus should a wild animal suddenly decide to join the party.

With the vodka soon showing its impact, all the officers descended from the bus with bravado, soon followed by the ladies. In no time, a locally arranged bonfire that had been rustled up to ward off the animals became the epicentre of enthusiastic song and dance. By about eleven that night, the party was in full swing, but by this time our would-be host for the evening had started getting worried at our non-arrival at his place, with no news from us, thanks to the

lack of mobile connectivity in the middle of the jungle. So, he sent out search and rescue teams, which managed to reach us around midnight after we sent word about our location through some vehicles that passed us. We eventually reached our host's mansion well past midnight, only to enjoy another rollicking party there with the local Indian community. Clearly, invoking the right mood on the right occasion and enjoying every situation regardless of the challenges is also an integral part of life's journey. Not to take away anything from the grand hospitality of our Indian hosts that night, the late evening 'in the middle of jungle' party with vodka, fafda and a bonfire was the winner all the way.

The Last Man Standing

In any war, it's the concept of the last man standing that decides who is the victor and who is the vanquished. In this context, the principle of the 'last man counts' is ingrained in a soldier at a very young age, right from the days of his recruit training, and amongst the officers at the pre-commission training academies such as the NDA and IMA. Accordingly, even during the most ferociously contested inter-squadron sports competitions, such as the cross-country or the endurance runs during field camps, the inter se standing of the squadron or the company is not decided by the first cadet or gentleman cadet but on the basis of the timing of the last cadet or gentleman cadet crossing the finish line. The team results are thus determined by the efforts of the last man. This principle of 'last man counts' at the NDA (also referred to as the Cradle of Leadership) acts as an incubator for nurturing the honour code of 'leaving no man behind'. The thumb rule in any military training is that more than the results, it is the efforts that signify the measure of one's achievements. If efforts are lacking during training, they will also be inadequate during an actual operation. This inculcation of the concept of 'last man counts' in the soldiers and officers is similar to the 'hip-pocket skill' elaborated by Indra Nooyi, the former CEO of PepsiCo. Anyone gaining proficiency in the specialized hip-pocket skill is categorized as an expert in that skill across the entire spectrum of all of one's operations in the organization. According to Ms Nooyi, developing a hip-pocket skill early in one's career paves the way for long-term success. She also suggests that this skill should be soft, not hard, and that it should be something that sets the person acquiring the skill apart from others. The principle of the 'last man counts' is thus akin to a soft hip-pocket skill that a soldier develops early in his career, and which he lives and dies by until the last day he wears the uniform.

To conclude this chapter, I must leave the readers with this apt quote about winning motives and victories:

> *'Men, money and material cannot by themselves bring victory or freedom. We must have the motive-power that will inspire us to [do] brave deeds and heroic exploits.'*
> —Netaji Subhas Chandra Bose

5

Goals, Dreams, Mindsets: Navigating Your Path

क्षिप्रं विजानाति चिरं शृणोति विज्ञाय चार्थं भजते न कामात् ।
नासम्पृष्टो व्यौपयुङ्क्ते परार्थे तप्रज्ञानं प्रथमं राजर्षिर्यस्य ॥

'That individual who understands effortlessly, heeds unwearyingly, pursues his objective with a keen sense of logic and not from desires or blind beliefs, is sure to be a person who has realized the greatest of wisdom and is therefore deserving of leadership.'

Achieving Dreams to Attain Success

Dare to Dream or Dare to Aim

'*A dream is not that which you see while sleeping, it is something that does not let you sleep.*' This rather unique description of a dream by one of the most popular Presidents of India, Dr A.P.J. Abdul Kalam, implies that one who dares to dream must have the passion and commitment to fructify those dreams into reality. Those who dare to dream must thus exhibit a firm resolve to move away from a restraining past and towards a fulfilling future.

As a soldier, I would be reticent to base real-life decisions on a dream that is actually a product of the subconscious mind, and would instead decide to adopt a realistic approach and deliberate with my team for achieving our goals. Even more significantly, failure to realize a dream would adversely affect the morale of both the leader and the team. Hence, as a leader of soldiers in combat, with due respect to President Kalam, I would prefer to replace the adage 'Dare to Dream' with the more pragmatic goal 'Dare to Aim', and simultaneously resolve to fulfil those aims with diligence and dedication.

Let me highlight a key distinction between the corporate world and the army, as for the CEO of a corporate house, the non-fulfilment of a dream would signify only a financial loss. In contrast, for a military commander, the failure to achieve a dream may imply the loss of his own life and/ or the lives of his soldiers, as well as ignominy for both his paltan and the nation. Thus, the ethos of military leadership dictates the setting of an achievable aim after deliberating all the pros and cons of the situation as against daring to dream big. Such a corporate strategy, coupled with the acumen to take calculated risks and optimize opportunities, would also pay better dividends, enabling the business house to effectively deal with competition. Taking calculated risks and exploiting fleeting opportunities are very much a part of setting achievable aims that are executed boldly.

Willpower Versus Wishful Thinking

'If wishes were horses, beggars would ride.' This age-old proverb can be interpreted both as the providential attainment of a heartfelt wish or the relentless willpower to achieve even a far-fetched wish. Very often we hear people say, 'I wish it

works out the way I hoped it would.' At the same time, we also hear some say, 'I will work it out the way I hoped to.' While the end-result in either case is the same, the means to achieve that end are conspicuously different, and herein lies the notable difference between a wish and the will to attain it. A 'wish' suggests a lack of agency as it represents the desire for things to somehow end up the way one wants, whereas 'will' signifies the power to take matters into one's hands and control the outcome by being in command of the situation. The operative term here is 'in command'. In the military, when commanders are 'in command' of an operation or a body of troops, it becomes not only their official responsibility but also a moral obligation to ensure the safety of the troops under their command while accomplishing the assigned mission.

A commander who is 'in command' of an operation does not have the luxury of wishing for the successful completion of an operation; instead they have to be hands-on and prudently orchestrate the employment and deployment of all the available resources to execute the operation as per plan. Taking the analogy further, the critical distinction between 'wish' and 'will' can therefore be explained as follows: a 'wish' or desire can imply the willing suspension of disbelief to aspire for something that may or may not be actually achievable; whereas 'will' or willpower presupposes various options, eventualities, strengths, weaknesses, challenges, assets, liabilities and, above all, the quality of leadership for converting the wish into reality.

A sardonic but pragmatic suggestion to all dreamers would be to consider 'hope' as a good breakfast but a bad supper. Rather than sustaining hope without initiating any action,

I would strongly advise all aspirants to 'get up, tie your laces and work actively to achieve your goals'. Taken intuitively, this assertion is a reiteration of one's self-worth and self-confidence that would drive action to channelize the will for realizing a wish. '*Kuchh toh log kahenge, logon ka kaam hai kehna* (people will say things, it's their job to say things)' are the lyrics of a famous Hindi song. There will always be someone who will not see your worth; don't let that someone be you.

Goals Versus Dreams

In the army, the task of laying down a plan for any given military situation, be it attack, defence, a counterterrorist operation or any other challenge, begins with listing out the terms of reference or non-negotiable directions, followed by writing down the objective of the operation in a single line. Thereafter, all the other aspects, such as the ground situation, the enemy, own troops, timings of the operation and various options need to be considered for delineating the most suitable plan to execute the operation according to the given terms of reference. This aim in the military appreciation can be likened to the goal or targets set by the leader for employees in a corporate environment. I would urge young readers to go through this section carefully as many of the youngsters I have interacted with on social media are ostensibly struggling to understand the concept of goals versus dreams.

Dr Neetinder Brar, founder of The Power With-In, transformational business, personal growth and mindset coach, speaker and corporate healthcare leader, points out the salient differentiation between goals and dreams. She opines that the basic reason why people's life goals are not attained is ironically because people do not have goals; they have dreams, desires and hopes but do not translate these into goals. Dr Brar offers the following words of wisdom to explain this mindset further:

Most people don't pursue their own goals at all. They follow what the world tells them is the best, easiest, most profitable (hopefully) thing to do.

Why don't people pursue their own dreams as goals? Because they believe they aren't good enough—this is the root of all things.

It's the conditioning of the masses—I'm not good enough for that big dream, I don't have enough knowledge, know enough people, have enough resources, etc., etc. Other people can do it but not me. I don't have the support, the guidance . . . bottom line: I'm not good enough.

Fear sets in and they take refuge in the phrase, 'You don't understand; my situation is different!'

And then the classic, 'I don't have time . . .'

No time for your dream? Whose life are you living?

The fact is these are simply dialogues in the head. Change the dialogue.

Your situation is not different, it's the same as millions of others, the fears and excuses too are the same. Stop saying this, it's your excuse.

When you change the thoughts you engage in, you change your beliefs, that changes how you feel and that makes you act differently and finally the results change.

As for time, everyone has the same twenty-four hours. What are you filling yours with?

Initiate this change.

Start by defining YOUR Goal—what do YOU want to achieve and by doing what (the service you intend to provide to reach your goal)?

What do YOU want? Not what your parents, spouse, children, friends think is good for you or the best thing to do.

Change your mental conditioning—you are more than good enough! It is not a lack of ability; it is a lack of belief, a fear that comes from wrong conditioning.

Fear is because we are ignorant of the processes and laws of success. Fear is just ignorance.

Need support? Get professional guidance. It's a goal, not a hobby.

Turning the dream into a goal is a process. First the dream has to be turned into an idea; then you look at the idea and ask, 'Am I capable?' And the answer is: 'Of course you are.' We all are.

But the more fundamental question is: 'Am I willing?' Now this is what it takes. Are you willing to do whatever it takes to reach your goal? That makes a dream a goal.

Once you commit, the 'Aim/Goal' is set and only then will the means open up, not before.

Start with this. Get mental clarity on 'what' you want before 'how' you can get it.

It will stop you from running in circles at the same place.

Believe in your dreams, turn them into goals and act without fear. Fear is tackled by intelligent and persistent action.

Will Versus Skill

The oft-repeated expressions, 'He/she is a willing worker' or 'He/she is a very skilled worker', are used to describe the work ethic of employees in an organization. The corresponding comment in the army is, '*Saab, XYZ datt ke naukri karne wala jawan hai* (XYZ soldier will stand firmly at his post without wavering from doing his assigned duty).' This is a

testimony to the character of a soldier, defining their steely nerves and will to hold on to their post till the 'last man last round' in the face of the enemy even in a scenario spelling certain death. As trained soldiers, they display an unassailable commitment and skill to perform the assigned task, come what may. This combination of training and willpower is what makes a soldier a truly dependable protector of the nation and its citizens. Such soldiers are those few good men the nation depends upon and the citizens are proud of.

Similar attributes are imparted to students in management schools, where they are taught the 'Skill Will Matrix'. This matrix is a 2×2 quadrant functioning as a coaching and assessment tool by juxtaposing a worker's willingness level against their degree of skill to accomplish a given task. Each quadrant specifies how a manager should engage with and manage the employees classified under the different quadrants. I must point out that while management schools teach this to managers as a 'mind thing', the military treats this as a 'heart thing' to be imbibed by its leaders and soldiers. The different quadrants of the matrix and their implications are detailed below.

	High will	
	High will / **Low skill**	**High will /** **High skill**
	Low will / **Low skill**	**Low will /** **High skill**
Low will		
	Low skill ⟷	High skill

Skill and Will Chart

Quadrant I: High Will, High Skill: A corporate manager will focus on training their skilful and motivated workers capable of optimally achieving their assigned targets. Concomitantly, leaders in the corporate world would prefer to delegate independent tasks to their competent employees, thereby allowing the latter certain autonomy in the implementation of projects. A military leader, on the other hand, would view a highly motivated junior as an asset whose time and efforts should not be wasted in routine activities that can well be performed by someone else. Thus, such troops, say 'special forces', would be employed in the most critical phase of an operation wherein their role could help turn the tide and change the course of the battle in favour of the own troops. Such employees are usually categorized as 'disruptive human resources', whose deployment can lead to disproportionate gains for the team.

Quadrant II: High Will, Low Skill: For a corporate manager, workers with a high degree of motivation but low skill set are capable of improving if provided due guidance and appropriate training over a period of time. However, since corporate managers usually lack the time and resources to individually train their promising employees, they often choose the easy way out by recruiting another person to do so instead. In the process, not only do they lose a highly motivated employee but also dampen the latter's self-esteem and passion for their job. A military leader, on the other hand, would assign such young soldiers to a highly experienced JCO in the most difficult phase of the operation where grit, mental toughness and human endurance would determine victory in the battle.

Such individuals can inspire other members of the team with their high motivation levels to achieve unprecedented results against all odds in highly demanding war situations.

This takes me back to the year 1986 when our battalion was stationed in the Lake City of Udaipur in Rajasthan. As a young second lieutenant, I was a member of the unit's basketball team that was scheduled to participate in the Inter-battalion Divisional Basketball Championship in Jamnagar, Gujarat. In the army, an officer is mandated to be a playing member of the team in all sports except contact sports like *kabaddi* or wrestling. Our team played exceptionally well to win the basketball competition, which was followed by the volleyball competition in Jamnagar itself. My unit dispatched the volleyball team to Jamnagar and asked me to stay back there to participate in the volleyball competition too as a mandatory playing member. Since I was a reasonably good volleyball player, the competition went off well.

The volleyball competition was followed by swimming, again in Jamnagar. Our unit had just moved from a high-altitude area in the eastern sector to Udaipur and there were no swimming pools at either of the two locations. Interestingly, everyone in the unit assumed that I must be a good swimmer too just because I could play the other games well. Therefore, my unit moved the swimming team to Jamnagar, asking me again to stay back with the team as the officer-in-charge. In addition to the normal individual and team swimming events (including water polo), we had to participate in the 4 x 100 metres officers' relay. My unit informed me that three other officers would reach the venue to join me on the day of the officers' relay event and that I would be the fourth member of the team. The catch here was that nobody asked me if I could swim 100 metres. In the NDA and IMA, the basic swimming test for successfully passing out from the academy entailed proficiency in the 55-metre breaststroke, which I had cleared only once in each academy with all the strength at my disposal.

Even as I was mulling over a strategy to handle this unexpected challenge, our team's JCO in-charge, Subedar Shanti Saran Singh, an extremely motivated soldier who had proved his mettle in the previous high-altitude field tenure, suddenly appeared in the role of a life-saver, assuring me that our team would win the competition with or without the officers' relay points. Refusing to be complacent, I got down to charting out a frenetic training schedule over the next four days, practising in the swimming pool at odd hours in the morning and late evenings to prepare for the event. I must confess that notwithstanding my best efforts, I could never reach the magical mark of 100 metres, falling short by 10–15 metres every time. On the given day, as the competition commenced, and true to the prediction by Subedar Shanti Saran Singh, the team assumed a leading position from the very first event. My apprehensions also diminished somewhat as the team continued its winning performance over the next two days of competition, with the officers' relay slated to be the culminating event on the third and final day of the competition. It was to be followed by the prize distribution ceremony, wherein the prizes would be presented by the local station commander, Brigadier J.S. Dhillon, a decorated soldier with an enviable military reputation, in the presence of all the officers and soldiers of Jamnagar station, along with their families.

As the event approached, cool and confident that we would wade through this formality to emerge winners,

I changed into my swimming trunks just before the commencement of the relay race. However, my self-assurance was rudely shattered as Subedar Shanti Saran Singh suddenly appeared from nowhere, brandishing a diary with some calculations in my face, according to which our team would become overall divisional champions only if we managed to finish the relay event to earn two points; and failure to complete the event would lead to our disqualification, earning us zero points and pushing the team down to the overall second position. The *subedar's* parting words, '*Saab, puri team ki izzat aapke upar nirbhar hai* (Sir, the entire team's reputation depends on you alone)', were still ringing in my ears as I looked woefully at the blue waters of the pool in the stadium. I had barely recovered from the shock inflicted by the subedar when I realized that the first three officers had completed their laps in the relay and it was my turn to jump into the pool. I was standing on the edge of the pool, wondering how to deal with this crisis when Subedar Shanti Saran Singh's high-pitched voice returned to torment me. Literally trying to escape his terrifying command, I jumped into the pool in a stupor and started swimming.

As the swimmers from the other teams swam spiritedly, touching the 50-metre end of the pool and returning rapidly for the next lap, I could hardly cover about 25 metres. But the cold water splashing on my face brought me back to my senses, and the loud cheers of the crowd started egging me on as by now, I was the only swimmer left in the pool. Huffing and puffing, I reached the halfway mark, then tried to gain distance on the return lap through a strong push against the wall. However, exhaustion was catching up, as I dragged both my mind and body towards what seemed a supremely unattainable goal. By now, I was reaching the stage wherein my body was slowing down but my mind was telling me to play it hard and don't give up. Desperately trying to avert drowning and stay afloat, I summoned whatever little energy I had left to somehow complete the race. The sight of a few kids cheering me on from the poolside reminded me that as an officer-in-charge and leader of the team, I could not fail my team under any circumstances.

Finally, as I finished the 100-metre lap with the last dregs of my mental and physical strength, I vowed that this swimming odyssey would be the first and last in my life. As our team won the 'Champions' trophy that day, it dawned on me that it was not '**skill**' but '**will**' that saved the day for us. During the barakhana held that evening to celebrate our team's victory, I was humbled as everyone ignored the winners of other events and walked up to congratulate me instead for what they termed as a 'heroic effort' against all odds that brought our team the overall championship title. I learnt my lesson that in a team event, individual skill is not that relevant but the unputdownable will is the single-most winning factor.

Quadrant III: Low Will, Low Skill: According to the management pamphlets, individuals with low skills and a low level of motivation need regular supervision and focused directions to be able to deliver better performance. This mandate is in conflict with the current widely prevalent principle of multitasking and cost-cutting, whereby companies strive to minimize the number of employees on their payroll, and can ill-afford to recruit extra employees merely to supervise other less-skilled employees. In the army, the leader may utilize the services of such soldiers in areas where the integrity and value

system of the individual would matter more than technical skills and motivation, especially in life-and-death situations. It is in such situations that the concepts of Wafadari, Imaandari, Zimmedari come to the fore, with such dyed-in-the-wool soldiers acting as a source of emotional strength for their compatriots in the objective of protecting and serving the nation. Further, a caring and compassionate leader would doubtlessly be a great motivator for other team members in situations where humanitarian qualities outweigh other considerations.

Quadrant IV: Low Will, High Skill: A corporate employee with a high level of good skills but a lack of motivation would be an asset only in an organization driven by high-end technology and challenging targets. In such a scenario, a corporate manager can assign tasks to employees based on their specific areas of specialization, simultaneously appreciating their work to keep their motivation alive. This quadrant is applicable in the military to the extent that the infusion of technology in warfare necessitates the recruitment of technical experts with high skills, who can be gainfully employed in the back-end operations such as research and development. The success of such employees in their respective fields of expertise, coupled with due recognition of their work, will motivate them to achieve higher goals.

Leadership Tactics and Strategies

Seeking Encounter
This strategy comes into play in counterterrorist operations, when the presence of terrorists is continuously being reported by intelligence sources in a particular area but the troops on ground are unable to locate them using traditional

techniques, such as 'search and destroy' or 'cordon and search', necessitating out-of-the-box thinking. I had discussed one such technique called 'swarming operations' in my earlier book, *Kitne Ghazi Aaye, Kitne Ghazi Gaye*. Without going into the tactical details, similarly, 'seeking encounter' is another such technique used by security forces to establish contact with terrorists when the latter prove elusive in certain difficult areas. The concomitant strategy in the corporate world can be categorized as 'seeking opportunities', wherein traditional business practices often need to be replaced by unorthodox solutions to combat competitors. Significantly, the most innovative ideas are often the brainchild of young, relatively inexperienced employees whose vision is not yet suppressed or coloured by orthodox practices.

When I, as a major general, was commanding a division on the western front, a lower formation had worked out an automated road movement model during a war-room discussion. This model was designed by senior officers with extensive experience of undertaking convoy movements in their military careers. However, this model was not working smoothly or providing the desired results. In order to break the impasse, I decided to engage young officers in the station with less than two years of military service, asking them to re-jig the model for better results. A young officer who had left the Indian Institute of Technology (IIT) after one semester to join the army asked me if the new team could re-work the model from scratch. Convinced that experienced inputs were integral for obtaining a correct output, the senior officers balked at this idea. Undeterred, the young officer said that the senior officers were using legacy data, whereas he wanted to incorporate a fresh logic and algorithm into the model. Seeing some value in his suggestion, I gave the young officers

a free hand and, sure enough, the outcome was a highly innovative working model that brought us some amazing results. This model thus became to war-room strategy what 'seeking encounter' is to field operations.

Importance of Discipline

The importance of discipline and rigorous implementation of the laid-out plan are two non-negotiable ingredients in any strategy, including the seeking encounter operations. A disclaimer here is that though discipline is the bedrock of any successful venture, youngsters today often do not appreciate operating within the constraints and confines of strict discipline codes and structures. Hence, the need for greater flexibility in their style of working, which should be supplemented with tremendous self-discipline. Individual whims leading to any act that jeopardizes the achievement of the organization's vision and goals or tarnishes its image cannot be accepted. Just as *paltan ki izzat* (honour of the regiment) is a non-negotiable code of honour, as mentioned in an earlier chapter, the corporate world, too, must promote values of integrity to protect the honour of the organization. I have seen some youngsters complaining about their bosses being 'hard taskmasters'. Having served in a highly disciplined force for nearly four decades, I would say that being a hard taskmaster is not an action; it's a feeling. And as long as the occasional feeling conveyed is in the interest of the team and organization for achievement of end goals, I will go by the dictum '*Jitna tapata hai sona, utna aata hai nikhar* (the more the gold is heated, the more it shines).'

Maintenance of Momentum

'Selection and Maintenance of the Aim' is one of the key principles of war. This is complemented by another principle, viz., 'Maintenance of the Momentum' in any given situation. This can be explained as achievement of one's objective through persistent application of one's fighting efforts, thereby preventing the enemy from recovering from any setbacks. In such cases, the army moves forward by pressing home the advantage of its initial successes, inspired by the motto, '*Fastest, Firstest and Fittest*' to maintain the momentum gained through their faster and more sprightly operations.

Habits of Eagle Leadership

Dr Roland F. DeRenzo, CEO at Colorado Springs Christian School, Colorado, USA, describes the difference between the unique habits of ducks and eagles when it comes to leadership. He lists out seven good characteristics of eagles that need to be understood by all students aspiring to become leaders. I discuss five of them here in relation to military leadership and their relevance in all walks of life.[4]

Eagles fly alone at high altitude: Successful leaders stay away from bickering and narrow-mindedness, especially in view of today's volatile social media environment. People you have in your life define you; so it's nice to have a great definition of yourself. Just as eagles prefer to keep the illustrious company of high-fliers and like-minded achievers, the company you keep also describes who you are and what you will become. The renowned poet Iqbal sums up this leadership trait in his couplet, '*Tu shaheen hai parwaaz hai kaam tera, tere saamne aasman aur bhi hain* (You are a falcon, flight is your vocation; you have many other skies to

---

[4] Source: Dr Roland DeRenzo, '7 Habits of Eagles Leadership', Colorado Springs Christian School, 15 February 2022, https://cscslions.org/dr-derenzo-s-blog/7-habits-of-eagles-leadership-lesson.

stretch your wings).' This trait of flying high requires strong physical stamina and mental endurance, as also graphically expressed in another couplet, '*Jiski jitni udaan baaki, utna uska asmaan baaki* (Your stamina to fly high will determine how many more skies you can conquer).'

Eagles have vision: As discussed above, organizational goals can be achieved only through prudent selection and meticulous adherence to one's aim, keeping in mind all the accompanying challenges. A leader who carefully considers all the available inputs and options thus usually makes the right decision.

Eagles are fearless: Since fear is the manifestation of normal human behaviour in mitigating circumstances, what is important is not to eliminate fear completely but to deal with it head-on and emerge stronger from the experience. Leaders must also remember that their team members derive strength from their courage and ability to overcome apprehensions. We will discuss how a military leader handles fear and failures later in the book.

Eagles are tenacious: As pointed out in an earlier chapter, a bison runs into the snowstorm instead of away from it. Similarly, an eagle flies into the storm and uses the strong headwinds to soar higher. Like eagles, successful leaders, too, face challenges fearlessly, even using them to beat opponents at their own game. Giving up is never an option for winners, and winning is never an option for those who give up. What really sets great leaders apart is their resoluteness in the face of adversity.

Eagles never feed on dead prey: Just as eagles ignore dead prey and instead seek newer targets to satisfy their hunger, great leaders, too, never talk about or rely on past glory but always

seek newer, unchartered territories to conquer. This attribute is aptly defined by the old African proverb, 'A cat that dreams of becoming a lion must lose its appetite for rats.' Soldiers fighting enemies to protect innocent citizens and firefighters who save lives by rushing into a fire seldom boast about their feats later.

Aim High, Attempt Higher, Achieve Highest

Happy Team: A leader willing to go the extra mile to ensure the success of a team is a true asset for the organization. In the words of Jimmy Carr, the noted British-Irish comedian and presenter, 'Happiness in achieving is expectations exceeded.' This implies that achievement of the anticipated results should not foment undue happiness, for it merely signifies the achievement of the set targets. Real joy should come when the team is empowered and works as a happy unit within a conducive environment, and their achievement goes beyond expectations.

Make a Difference: Making a difference through one's efforts goes beyond fulfilling one's duty or accomplishing the assigned tasks. It's actually about touching someone's heart and soul and making a difference in their lives. Being part of someone's journey does not necessarily mean that you are the pusher or a puller to help them reach their destination; you can just be a non-contributory bystander like a milestone on the roadside whose sheer presence and visibility every few seconds gives the traveller the feel of accomplishment and success on their journey. A leader could thus also aim to achieve the significant goal of becoming a meaningful part

of someone's life, personifying the sentiment that they will 'always be there for you'.

Adopt a Winning Mindset: Since failure is a better teacher than success, leaders need to be prepared to fall multiple times and rise after each setback by banking on their grit and endurance to persevere in adversity. This ability to bounce back from challenges is what actually defines a leader, sifting the wheat from the chaff. A 'winning mindset' presupposes strong mental attributes needed for strategizing for the future while also analysing and learning from the pitfalls of the past, which is another critical aspect of military operations. Here, I would advise all potential leaders to overcome their feelings of insecurity and shun negativity, while striving to become the rock that withstands the wrath of all external elements and still stays firmly anchored in the earth. It is this rootedness and resilience that exemplifies the true mettle of a leader, and is literally the bedrock of the winning mindset.

> *'Don't take rest after your first victory because if you fail in the second, more lips are waiting to say that your first victory was just luck.'*
> —Dr A.P.J. Abdul Kalam

6

Navigating Crises with the Perspective of Strength and Wisdom

यथाशक्ति चिकीर्षन्ति यथाशक्ति च कुर्वते !
न किंचिदवमन्यन्ते राजर्शि:

*'They who exert their best of might, and also act to the best
of the strength, and disregard no threats as insignificant,
are most certainly the wise and have great potential in
them to be just leaders.'*

Is 'Managing' a Crisis Different from 'Navigating' a Crisis?

A crisis can be defined as 'a period or situation of intense difficulty or danger'. In other words, a crisis signifies an extraordinary social, economic, political or circumstantial upheaval in the life of an organization or individual.

In a corporate, a crisis may erupt due to various factors, including market instability, natural disasters, compromising of organizational reputation or image, issues with the nature or behaviour of the company's product(s), rise in competition or any other condition that would adversely affect the company's financial situation.

Financial losses in an organization can usually be recovered by professionally managing and assessing the crisis, analysing the causes and resetting the operational directives over a period of time. This option is, however, not available in the military, where mishandling of a crisis in a combat situation would invariably result in the loss of lives or ceding of national territory that may be difficult or impossible to recover. Therefore, handling of any crisis in the military is a far more complex and challenging task as compared to the way in which a crisis is '*managed*' in other organizations. The army works on the principle of a 'response mechanism' to a crisis by the entire team, including the commanders at all levels. This response mechanism is neither a knee-jerk reaction nor firefighting to resolve an unbidden problem but is actually an integral part of the process of 'navigating a crisis', including visualizing, planning, refining, war-gaming and executing a game plan to exploit the fleeting opportunities and the vulnerabilities of opponents; and finally institutionalizing short- and long-term measures to avert similar crises in the future. So yes, 'navigating' a crisis is different from 'managing' a crisis.

Options, Priorities and Choices

While navigating a crisis, the leadership in corporate boardrooms generally analyses the reasons for the setback and its impact. While identifying the available means and methods to recover losses, it prioritizes the available options and finally selects the main or most viable option; the single most important and deciding factor of viability being the commercial implications. In the army, on the other hand, the priority to defend the nation and safeguard

the lives of soldiers at any cost, overrides all other options for the commander, thereby virtually negating the financial aspect. Accomplishing one's mission is thus not only a non-negotiable mandate but literally the raison d'être for an army leader. When working on options and priorities, one 'prioritizes' what suits the situation the most from amongst a variety of available 'options'. 'Choice', on the other hand, is the only course of action irrespective of any other reason or consideration; and one will always 'choose' only this course under all circumstances and then make it work. A lover may say that they do not want to be an option but a priority; I would say if someone loves you, you have to be a conscious and only 'choice'; neither an option nor a priority. Similarly, in a crisis combat situation where one may have multiple options and priorities, a leader will always choose to save the lives of soldiers at all costs while keeping the accomplishment of the mission as non-negotiable. When in love, make a conscious 'choice' and never settle for an option or priority, period.

The Perspective of Strength

The strengths-based approach signifies a perspective that articulates the known or hidden power of individuals, families and communities to exhibit resilience and courage in the face of extreme adversity and succeed. The concept was formally articulated in 1989 by Ann Weick and her colleagues at the KU School of Social Welfare.[5] However, it can originally be traced back to the work of African American scholars and social workers, including W.E.B. Du Bois and Birdye Henrietta

---

[5] Source: 'History of Strengths Perspective at KU', KU School of Social Welfare, https://socwel.ku.edu/history-strengths-perspective.

Haynes. The concept is based on the argument that total commitment to one's mission and the power of self-belief and knowledge foster mental prowess and self-confidence, while building a positive mindset in the individual who nurtures such inner strength. It is this very strength that comes to the fore when a military leader takes on a mission and assumes charge of a team for fulfilling that mission. According to Shikha Pandey, a Mumbai-based mindfulness mindset coach, strength without compassion merely represents ego, whereas compassion for one's team members and concern for their well-being define the true strength of a leader.

An example from nature beautifully embodies this concept of deriving strength from within and through a shared goal. It has been scientifically proven that a sunflower looks up to the sun to imbibe energy (which is also reflected in its name). However, on a rainy or cloudy day when the sun is not visible, sunflowers turn to each other to absorb their mutual energy. This unique characteristic underscores the organic strength present deep within all living things, which imparts energy and vigour to other members of one's team. Sunflowers take the energy from the sun because the sun has the energy or strength but when they turn to the next flower for an exchange of energy, it is because they both believe that they have what it takes to be as strong as the sun. In a team, each member takes motivation and energy from their leader to outperform their own previous best performance. However, a good team member can always fill up for the leader in their absence and it works for both. This concept of compassion in the military, which extends to the level where a soldier will not shy away from laying down their life to save a team member, popularly known as the 'buddy system', is an unwritten rule and an intrinsic part of army life.

Wisdom of Knowing

One of the preconditions for handling a crisis is the wisdom and keen awareness about the situation exhibited by the leader. Chanakya, aka Kautilya, devotes special attention to this aspect of leadership in his *Arthashastra*, arguing that 'everything is a pain without the wisdom, and everything is bliss with wisdom'. Kautilya's centre of attention remains on knowledge and wisdom of a leader and he believes that effective leaders are the wise ones, first and foremost. He alludes to such a leader as *Rajarshi* or the wise one, an ideal leader or a sage-like king, who deserves the position of leadership.

This idea was also succinctly expressed by the highly respected cavalry officer, Lieutenant General T.S. Shergill, Param Vishisht Seva Medal (Retd), and former commandant of the Indian Military Academy, when he said in one of his talks, 'The limit of an Indian soldier is the limit of his officer.' From the perspective of leadership, this implies that a military commander's tactical abilities, strategic awareness and knowledge of the enemy's vulnerabilities and capabilities, combat experience, physical endurance, mental toughness and wisdom to choose the harder right instead of the easier wrong, as enshrined in the NDA prayer, will earn him the title of a leader. This will dictate his decisions and strategies at every step throughout his military career and also define the limits of achievements of the soldiers he commands in war or conflict situations.

Similarly, in a corporate scenario, the wisdom and awareness levels of a CEO shape his commitment to the organization's vision and core values, and how he and his team deal with both success and failure in their projects.

In the end, resilience in the face of adversity, pragmatism, empathy, ethical work culture, owning failures and crediting the team with success makes a leader. I recall an incident that occurred in North Kashmir during the days of intense terrorist activity in 2010–12, when I, as a brigadier, was commanding a Rashtriya Rifles sector in the region. We were engaged in a chance encounter with Pakistani terrorists in the dense jungles, and one of our teams injured two of them but they managed to escape due to the heavy undergrowth and poor visibility. One of our soldiers was also injured in that operation and was immediately evacuated to the Base Hospital in Srinagar by a helicopter. I met him at the helipad and expressed concern at his injury just before he was flown out. When I inquired as to how he was feeling, he did not reply to my question; instead, he smiled faintly, trying to hide his pain and said, '*Saab, mujhe maloom hain aap unko maar loge* (Sir, I know you will eliminate them).' At the risk of sounding immodest, I must say that these words evocatively express a soldier's confidence in the military acumen and wisdom of his leader.

We were able to prevent the injured terrorists from moving out of the area by rigorously checking all vehicular movement, especially because the encounter site was very close to the Line of Control and hence had very sparse civilian population. We were also aware that the terrorists could not go to a hospital for treatment and would instead seek treatment at the house of some local overground worker or a terrorist sympathizer. Armed with this background knowledge, I tasked my informers to keep an eye on the movements of all local 'compounders' (unqualified or under-trained nursing assistants who move from village to village to treat minor injuries or ailments) in the area. The

remote area had only three such individuals and their continued surveillance led us to the location of the hiding terrorists, who were being treated by one of these compounders. In a swift operation that followed the inflow of intelligence from my informers, we hunted down these terrorists within two weeks and eliminated them in a fierce gunfight. After the successful operation, my deputy sector commander, Colonel Prashant S. Nikam, who had been awarded the Sena Medal for gallantry twice, asked me why I had been so determined to track down and neutralize these two terrorists. My response was simple, 'I had to justify the belief that my injured soldier had in my wisdom and knowledge.'

Profit-Loss Statement

A Profit-Loss Statement (PLS) is usually prepared at the end of each month, quarter and year in every business house. Profit reflected in the PLS is usually celebrated enthusiastically across the organization, often being accompanied by awarding the title of 'Employee of the Month' to the person who made the most significant contribution to the profits. However, if the PLS shows a loss, what follows is a detailed analysis and a reworking of the strategy to make good the losses in successive time periods. In contrast, the army does not have this opportunity or luxury of making good the losses in successive operations, for a soldier's PLS cannot wait for the end of the month, quarter or year—it is prepared every second as long as he is part of an operation on the battlefield or elsewhere. The loss of a soldier is final and irrevocable, and can never be recovered for either his team or his family. A soldier is in profit when his buddy and he are safe and the enemy is suffering losses. The next moment, his buddy or he can get killed or injured, bringing them into loss instantly. And a soldier's loss cannot be recouped next month.

His loss is for eternity and those who are going to bear this loss for centuries to come may not even be aware or anywhere close to the place where the loss occurred. I am reminded of Muzaffar Razmi's famous couplet, '*Ye jabr bhi dekha hai, taarikh ki nazron ne, lamhon ne khata ki thi, sadiyon ne saza payi*', broadly translating as, 'Many injustices have been witnessed by the eyes of history, wherein for a mistake made in a moment, centuries have been punished.'

Navigating the Crisis

Mental Preparation: 'Well begun is half done' is an age-old wisdom quote. On different occasions, Steve Jobs and Nabil Sabio Azadi are supposed to have said, 'When fishermen can't go to sea, they repair nets.' The process of navigating a crisis sets in much before an actual crisis hits. Thus, cultivating the mental make-up to face minor obstacles is the first step towards handling any crisis. Navigating the challenges in life will always seem easy and smooth but one must remember that it is like climbing a pyramid, wherein only the fittest and fastest will reach the pinnacle. Further, the climbers need to remind themselves that every level presents a new challenge, and only renewed determination will take them to the top. In the army too, every operation is treated differently as each one differs from the other in terms of the enemy, terrain, weather, time of the year, composition of the team and the accuracy of the information available. While the physical planning and preparation for a specific operation commences only after the intelligence is received, the mental preparation to launch it commences much before the unit enters the specified area. The Indian Army also works on the premise that one's capabilities are always stronger than one's apprehensions. Building capabilities takes time; intentions can change in the wink of an eye. These

capabilities are honed through structured, non-structured and on-the-job training that help the soldier inculcate not only psychological, emotional and physical toughness but also self-belief and belief in the team and commander. Operational challenges will differ in every situation but these beliefs will help overcome them with relative ease. The adage, '**The more you sweat in peace, the less you bleed in war**' is inscribed on the entrance gates of all the training institutions of the Indian Army. It is this preparation that enables the army to handle not only combat situations but also natural disasters or man-made calamities, wherein army personnel are requisitioned to assist the civil administration at the last moment. The army at that moment cannot turn around and say that it is not prepared or equipped to do this task as it was preparing and training only for their primary task of fighting the enemy or terrorists. On the battlefield or away from it, in military operations or civil crises, the army always rises to the occasion to perform the assigned task with utmost professionalism. Just because the army does it well every time does not mean it is an easy job. This reminds me of the saying, 'Just because someone carries it well doesn't mean it isn't heavy.' This mental preparation over and above physical training to deal with any unknown impending situation or challenge is a key takeaway that corporate houses can imbibe from the army. In this context, the dictum, 'We will cross the bridge when we come to it', may not always be the best training motto for either the army or any corporate organization, especially in a high-stakes operating environment.

Planning and Preparation: Basic military training is designed to prepare soldiers for all types of warfare in different terrains. However, before being deployed in a particular operational area, such as high altitudes, jungles or

locations of counterterrorism movements, the troops and officers have to undergo specialized pre- and post-induction training in order to build on their mental and operational preparation. Similarly, corporate houses, too, need to prepare in advance for any crisis that may confront the organization. This planning and preparation entail the infusion of the following attributes in each team member:

- **Foresight**: This implies that the likely unfolding of events must be visualized in advance and take into account all the potential hurdles and roadblocks that may arise during the execution.
- **Analysis**: Appreciating or analysing the likely combat situation in a war room is the first and foremost step in preparing for a particular military operation. The major factors to be analysed include the non-negotiable terms of reference, ground realities as they exist in the area of likely operations and how the same can be used to one's own advantage, the enemy's strengths and weaknesses, own strengths and vulnerabilities and other extraneous factors such as the weather and logistics.
- **Flexibility**: It is prudent to remember that the adversary, too, indulges in planning and preparation, which is why no enemy would allow one's operations to progress as per plans envisaged during peacetime in the war rooms. Therefore, one's plans should be flexible enough to take into account any unexpected twist in the tale and should cater for extra resources and efforts to achieve the flexibility.
- **Contingency Planning**: It is a by-product of flexibility in planning. While being watertight in taking all eventualities into consideration, a plan should also

be amenable to modification or mid-course correction necessitated by an unforeseen contingency. It is therefore important to war-game all likely contingencies that may come up during the execution phase.

- **Ear to the Ground**: An unspoken rule in the military is that it is not enough to just make a plan and then wait complacently for a favourable situation to put it into action. Keeping oneself abreast of all news about the enemy's latest positions and manoeuvres, and accordingly modifying one's plans is a continuous process. Hence, all available intelligence sources must always remain activated to know the latest about the enemy. In a corporate scenario, too, teams and their leaders need to continuously monitor the evolving market dynamics, consumer choices, competitors' activities and new products entering the market, and accordingly update their own strategies.

- **Keep it Simple, Silly (KISS)**: All plans in the army are devised while keeping in mind the reality that at any point of time, they may need to be executed by junior officers, such as a section commander (*havildar*), platoon commander (subedar saab) or company commander (captain or major) on the ground. Strategists in a corporate environment, too, need to realize that all the elaborate plans made by them may have to be implemented on the ground by their subordinates such as interns in the marketing, sales and production departments. Hence, it is imperative to keep these plans simple and easy to implement, a reality aptly described by the army precept, 'Keep it Simple, Silly', and its perspicacious acronym, KISS!

- **Reserves**: A back-up plan or Plan B can be effectively executed by a military leader only if sufficient reserves of troops and materials, including weapons and equipment, are commissioned and available for deployment in operations as and when the need arises. Another non-negotiable aspect is that reserves, once committed, must be immediately recreated; meaning at no stage of the battle should a commander be without reserves. The concomitant reserves for a corporate leader, on the other hand, entail access to liquid funds, advice and guidance from experts, and the wherewithal to handle any adversity with equanimity. Ideal leaders in both army and civilian roles must, therefore, embody experience, knowledge and acumen to both command and gain the trust of their team members.

Execution: A plan is only as successful as its execution, and effective implementation of the plan largely depends on the capability of the leader. Crisis management (yes, immediate managing is one part of navigating the crisis) under an adverse situation is the hallmark of a leadership test. A leader must, at all times, remain calm, composed and visibly in control even under the most adverse situation. During my multiple tenures in Kashmir, there were numerous incidents when our teams came under terrorist fire, and one or more of our soldiers were hit without warning by their bullets. In such incendiary scenarios, a leader needs to broadly follow these steps:

- **No Halts**: In the army, the team on the ground continues the operation without allowing any respite to the terrorists, as the task in hand must never be compromised at the altar of any crisis.

- **Limit the Damage**: The immediate job of the core team under fire is to limit the damage caused by the crisis by taking immediate steps, such as administering first aid and continuing to engage the terrorists with a heavy volume of fire to avoid further damage. In a military operation, while the core team continues to focus on the main objective, a small sub-team is constituted to execute the peripheral tasks such as shifting the injured to a safer place until the arrival of the medical team.

- **Save**: After limiting the initial damage and evacuating the casualties to the nearest hospital, the next step is to save the injured soldiers by providing them the best possible medical care. Similarly, in a corporate scenario, experts are commissioned to tackle and recoup losses emanating from a crisis that hits the organization or any of its projects. In other words, the corporate brings in experts to analyse and pinpoint what went wrong and these experts suggest how things can be fixed; something akin to appointing a fact-finding mission.

- **Assess**: After having absorbed the initial impact, the core team reassesses the situation and modifies the plan to be able to regain the moral ascendency and complete the mission, often with the use of the reserves at their disposal.

- **Re-analyse**: If the local actions by the core team have not produced the desired results, it is at this stage that a fresh analysis of the emerging situation is carried out at a higher level, considering the damage already caused and ability to absorb further damage. This assessment is based on a SWOT analysis of both the adversary and one's own resources.

- **Strike**: The review process is followed by implementation of a revised plan to ensure success with a final all-out effort.

Should! Would! Could! . . . Did

The above process of planning and execution can be more adroitly visualized through the example of an incident that occurred during the winter of 2019 in the snow-covered hills of South Kashmir, where a small army team was engaged in an intelligence-based operation. After trudging through the snow the entire night, the team managed to reach the likely hideout of the terrorists undetected. The area, covered by thick and tall pine trees, was cordoned off by positioning four to five buddy pairs around it, while a hit team of four soldiers led by the commander himself closed in on the target. Suddenly, the hit team came under fire from a terrorist who spotted them when he was out to relieve himself. As one of the soldiers was injured and the team had already lost the element of surprise, the operation had to be reviewed urgently. The commander had the Hobson's choice of pulling back and regrouping or risking more casualties by going ahead with the plan in the face of the terrorist's persistent firing. In this ambivalent situation, a young soldier, deployed as part of the cordon, showed incredible presence of mind, shifting his position and sliding down in the snow for 20 metres, without waiting for any further orders from the commander. His buddy, who was his senior, followed suit, with both of them reaching a spot from where they could successfully fire at the terrorist and knock him down, thereafter giving an all-clear signal to the hit team. This entire action took place in the span of less than a minute, giving no time to the terrorists inside the hideout to

react. Leaving one of the soldiers in the team to look after the injured, the commander moved ahead towards the hideout with his buddy, swiftly neutralizing the remaining terrorists. Here, though the initial plan was compromised, Plan B was successfully executed by a soldier who reviewed the situation within seconds, and took immediate action to strike, thereby saving lives and limiting the damage. This episode also underscores the importance of combining courage and quick thinking with experience and maturity to achieve success. As a leader, one should never underestimate the contribution of the most inexperienced team member who may well be the catalyst for success in a given situation.

Avoiding Recurrence

Restore: The process of handling a crisis or an adverse situation does not end with its successful management. In fact, one of the most important aspects of navigating a crisis is going back to its genesis, and restoration is the first step of that process, implying that the situation should first be restored to what it was before the advent of the crisis.

Reset: This step entails analysing the reasons for the crisis and plugging all the loopholes to prevent its recurrence. Resetting means carrying out certain organizational or structural changes in the techniques or technologies to ensure better future outcomes by reducing the potential for similar crises, without compromising the vision and set goals of the organization.

Restart: Once the causes of the crisis have been identified and addressed, it is in the best interest of the organization to eliminate all threats and weed out those responsible for the crisis without any regrets, guilt or remorse, as a character in the famous American television drama series *Game of Thrones* says, 'Wars teach people to obey the sword, not the gods.'

Refocus: Refocusing is the art of changing mindsets by forgetting the past and working together for a better future. For this purpose, any previous linkages with people or procedures associated with the crisis need to be discontinued or else they could come back to foment another crisis. The renowned and highly respected industrialist Ratan Tata is famously quoted as having said, 'None can destroy iron, but its own rust can. Likewise, none can destroy a person, but their own mindset can.' **Talking about refocus, the most difficult job for a military leader is to salute his comrade for the one last time and probably the most honourable job is to get back to the mission at hand with renewed focus as a tribute to the fallen soldier.**

Review: Last but not least, in most organizations, especially where functionaries are frequently transferred, as in the military, there is a tendency to overlook past mistakes and the lessons learnt from them remain buried in the files until the next crisis strikes. In such a context, it is imperative to regularly review and update the standard operating procedures (SOPs) to ensure avoidance of future crises. The organizations with the most talented teams can be unsuccessful if their talent doesn't keep the lessons of the past close to their heart. Asking for help when in a difficult situation is not a sign of weakness. The importance of learning from the past comes forth in the following conversation in Charlie Mackesy's popular book, *The Boy, the Mole, the Fox and the Horse*:

'What is the bravest thing you've ever said?' asked the boy.
'Help,' said the horse.
'Asking for help isn't giving up,' said the horse. 'It's refusing to give up.'

Acknowledging and rectifying past mistakes is the first step in the process of seeking help. It is also important to remember that successful people have the most bruised shoulders and the burden of responsibility of someone's faith is probably the heaviest.

Emotional Strength

Mumma, Please Don't Tell Dad: I would like to conclude this chapter by recounting a real-life incident (the names of individuals and places have been changed for privacy reasons). This is not related to operations but reflects the emotional strength of a soldier's family, which in turn, inspires a soldier to make any sacrifice for the country that he serves till his last breath. The story, dating back to late 1999, was narrated to me by an officer, Major Singh, who was posted somewhere in the Western region at that time. One of his junior officers, Captain Anjali, was married to Captain Ganesh, a professional officer, posted in the Northern theatre. Ganesh got injured during the Kargil War and as per the existing army procedures, a medical board conducted checks and declared him medically fit to continue in service and perform all military duties. The day Captain Ganesh came to know of the outcome of his medical board proceedings, however, tragically proved to be his last as he passed away in his sleep due to an accident caused by the *bukhari* (coal room heater). When Major Singh received the news of this sad incident, he visited Captain

Anjali, along with his wife, to break the news to her and their toddler daughter Rani. Anjali accepted the news very bravely. After the initial period of grief, on her parents' persuasion, Anjali agreed to marry another army officer, Major Kumar. However, Rani was never told about her real father and she grew up as the daughter of Kumar and Anjali. Major Kumar and Anjali's own child was born several years after their marriage, as they wanted to devote maximum attention to their elder daughter Rani. Once Rani turned eighteen, Anjali decided to inform her that Kumar was not her real father. When she tearfully broke the news to Rani, she was amazed to see how well Rani took the news. Rani consoled her sobbing mother, saying, 'Mumma, please don't tell dad that I know the truth. In reality, I am his daughter.' Her maturity beyond her years showed how Rani had the best values of a military upbringing instilled in her since birth. Even more than her parents, she was actually the one who 'wore the boots'. Rani is a doctor now and continues to share a deep bond with her father Manoj.

> *'A country's greatness lies in its undying ideals of love and sacrifice that inspire the mothers of the race.'*
> —Sarojini Naidu

7

Adaptive Leadership: Who Truly Owns Your Organization?

न हृष्यन्तयात्मसंमाने नावमानेन तप्यते गाङ्गो हृद
इवाक्षोभ्यो यः स राजर्षिः उच्यते ।

*'They, who are never overwhelmed by pride, even on
receiving highest honours, and those who remain relaxed
and un-agitated like a lake in the course of the Ganga,
even amid the greatest of their crises, are verily the wise.
Only such individuals are deserving of the position
of leadership.'*

Adaptive Leadership

'Adaptive Leadership' is defined as a practical and
collaborative leadership style wherein leaders are
flexible in their approach and responsive to the needs of
their organizations, while working with their teams to create
solutions enabling organizations to adapt to changing times
and evolving situations that may lead to adversity and/or
tough competition. The operative words in this definition
are 'practical and collaborative leadership'. Adaptive leaders
are expected to anticipate foreseeable criticalities, have the
ability to visualize challenges and identify the reasons for their
emergence that will help in mitigating them.

Risk calculation, risk avoidance and risk absorption are among the most significant attributes of an adaptive leader. In simple terms, this amounts to evaluating what risks are worth taking and if the organization or the team has the bandwidth to bear those risks. Risk avoidance is the simplest and safest bet but then nobody ever became great by avoiding risks. **By not risking anything, you are actually risking everything.** Adaptive leaders are flexible in their approach and readily accept suggestions or feedback. They are also willing to change or realign their approach by carrying out mid-course corrections, where needed. The most important ingredient for carrying out feedback-based mid-course correction is the inherent flexibility in the plan as discussed in the previous chapter. This also entails admitting one's mistakes that may have been made inadvertently or in good faith and then making every effort to rectify those mistakes, which is the hallmark of an adaptive leader. Unless one accepts a mistake, one will never be able to get down to addressing it. It is pertinent to mention here that accepting a mistake comes with the added pressures of responsibility, accountability and the resultant blames.

Leaders should also refrain from assigning blame for errors on team members, as that amounts to offering excuses rather than looking for solutions. I remember offering the following explanation, '**We took it on our chin**', when during a press conference on 19 February 2019, we were questioned about the high number of casualties suffered by our security forces in the operation where they successfully eliminated the Pakistani terrorist organization Jaish-e-Mohammad's module within 100 hours of the latter carrying out the improvised explosive device (IED) blast at Pulwama. The

Indian security forces suffered casualties because the terrorists had been hiding in civilian houses and the security forces did not want to cause any collateral damage to the lives or property of innocent people.

Here I would like to cite another example away from the military domain. I remember a professor telling me that a famous singer used to maintain a personal diary in her childhood. In one of her entries, she wrote, '*When* I am successful . . .', not '*If* I am successful . . .' This positive attitude demonstrated as a child highlights the single biggest factor that determines the success of such personalities in adulthood, irrespective of the path they choose in life. When my debut book *Kitne Ghazi Aaye, Kitne Ghazi Gaye* was released, I had promised that I would personally sign all the copies pre-ordered on a leading online selling platform. I signed more than 12,000 copies over three days while sitting at the printing press. The signed copies were then dispatched to the distributors and online selling platforms to be sent to the readers who had pre-ordered. Since the popularity of the book exceeded everyone's initial estimates, the sellers asked for a higher number of copies, anticipating that the book would be sold out. In order to maintain an uninterrupted supply of books with the sellers, my publisher, Penguin Random House India, immediately released additional unsigned copies for the sellers a few days prior to the actual date of the release. However, due to some handling issues, the signed and unsigned copies got mixed up somewhere. Consequently, some readers who had pre-ordered the signed copies ended up receiving the unsigned copies and others who ordered after the release got the signed copies. I learnt about this mix-up when some readers raised the issue with me on social media. I discussed this with the publishers and both of us decided to honour my promise to the readers who had committed to purchase the book before its release. Immediately swinging into action, the publishers sent the signed copies to all the readers who were supposed to get the signed copies without replacement or return of the unsigned copy, without charging any money from the author, that's me. These efforts by the publishers and their timely decision to counter the inadvertent mistake that perhaps occurred at the warehouse is a perfect example of adaptive leadership and its flexibility in responding to an unbidden crisis. I often cite this example involving corporate work ethics to underscore the fact that adaptive leadership is not the domain of the military alone. However, the subtle difference between the army and civil situations is that in the military, this ethos is followed as a thumb rule, whereas in a corporate, it depends on the situation and the individual in charge. A disclaimer that needs to be given is that there are no runners-up in war. Every fight for an army man is fought to win, with the stakes being life or death.

The Implications of Adaptive Leadership for a Soldier

Adaptive leadership comes naturally for a military leader because he is mandated to lead with a high degree of human interface and humane values, which form the backbone of military honour codes. The most conspicuous aspects of military leadership involve making split-second decisions and influencing the outcome of combat situations to ensure the success and safety of their troops. A split-second decision is not to be confused with a hasty decision; because a hasty decision presupposes not having considered all the relevant pros and cons and it may result in a terrible failure. This ability of a leader to make split-second

decisions comes with years of experience, self-confidence, faith in the capabilities of the team and awareness of the strengths and weaknesses of both one's own team as well as the opponents'. No plan is great unless it succeeds and the junior leaders executing it on the ground make it succeed with their grit and blood, not that of the war-room planners, whose well-thought-of plans often do not pass muster in a dynamic situation on the battlefield. The well-thought-of versus split-second-decision debate will always go in the favour of the leader executing the plan, who is mentally flexible and open to modification of his plans. A well-considered plan, if executed audaciously with the flexibility to be modified, can produce unprecedented results. An oft-repeated adage in the military is that most well-laid-out plans fail to survive the first bullet once the battle is joined. As a military leader who has also been entrusted with the responsibility of producing future leaders, I would say that any success I achieved was always due to the efforts of my team; and any failure, if and ever it happened, was because of some deficiency in my leadership. Positive mindset is the key to be an adaptive leader. Wafadari or loyalty is a key component of true leadership, as it includes the willingness to risk everything, including one's own life, for attaining the organizational goals and upholding the country's prestige. I quote below from an editorial article by Lt Col Dilbag Singh Dabas (Retd), titled, 'A Soldier's Creed Is a Class Apart', published in the *Tribune*, dated 9 January 2025, mentioning Subedar Richhpal Ram, Victoria Cross (Posthumous) of my unit, 4th Battalion The Rajputana Rifles:[6]

---

[6] Source: Lt Col Dilbag Singh Dabas (Retd), 'A soldier's creed is a class apart', *Tribune*, 9 January 2025, https://www.tribuneindia.com/news/musings/a-soldiers-creed-is-a-class-apart/.

When World War II broke out in 1939, Subedar Richhpal Ram of 4 Rajputana Rifles was on two months' leave at his village Barda in Gurgaon district. Barda was known in the region as 'Faujion ka gaon' since almost every household had at least one member who was serving or had served in the defence services. Soon after the war started, most faujis on leave in the village received recall telegrams one after another. They cut short their leave and returned to their paltans (battalions). Upset due to the non-receipt of a telegram for many days, Subedar Richhpal unilaterally decided to rejoin his paltan. Janaki, his wife, told him to wait, but he argued that the telegram meant for him had perhaps been wrongly addressed or got misplaced in transit. He insisted that his soldier's creed demanded his service and it was time for him to prove his wafadari towards his paltan and his country. During his send-off at the tonga stand, Richhpal said to his wife, '*Main ultoa aungo, morcho jeet ke aaungo. Aur jai ulto na aa payo to iso kuchh karjango ke mhari poori baradari tere pe garv karegi* (I will return victorious. But if I don't come back, I would have done something for which our entire clan will be extremely proud of you).' Sadly, he did not return from the war, but he kept his promise. He was posthumously awarded the Victoria Cross. Fast-forward to the middle of 1999, when the war clouds were gathering over Kargil. Some officers and jawans of the 17 Jat battalion were on leave. Realizing the operational urgency, the battalion adjutant, Major H.S. Madan, started sending recall telegrams. Major Deepak Rampal, Delta Company commander, 17 Jat, was on long leave, preparing for the staff college exam scheduled for September 1999. Unwilling to disturb Major Rampal during his

preparations, the commanding officer, Col U.S. Bawa, thought of sending a recall notice to him later, when the war became imminent. Col Bawa was pleasantly surprised when he saw Major Rampal, carrying a rucksack, walk into the battalion's operational room. When asked what made him rejoin without receiving the recall telegram, he replied, 'Sir, I heard on the radio news about Pak infiltration in the Kargil sector. I also read in the newspaper about the missing patrol of 4 Jat led by Lt Saurabh Kalia and the torture inflicted upon him and his men. I also saw coffins of our soldiers being brought to their villages. Did I need to know more and see more to take a decision?' Within a fortnight of his rejoining the battalion, Major Rampal led his Delta Company during an assault on the formidable Whale Back feature strongly held by Pakistani troops. After a fierce night-long fight, including hand-to-hand combat, the Whale Back was back in Indian hands. Major Rampal received a well-deserved Vir Chakra. Not just Richhpal and Rampal, all Indian soldiers have always been like that—a class apart. For them, their country and their paltan are supreme. Leave is too small a privilege for them.

Active Intelligence and Active Listening

I would urge readers to delve further into the concepts of Active Intelligence and Active Listening if they want to enhance their power of adaptive leadership. Active intelligence can be defined as a state of continuous intelligence or insight where processes support a need to act immediately based on real-time data. Since adaptive leadership requires a hands-on approach for navigating any crisis by taking timely decisions based on the evolving situation, accessing updated and continued intelligence is a precondition for taking a win-win decision. Active listening, on the other hand, goes beyond merely hearing words to fully focusing on understanding, assimilating and responding to what is being said by being fully present in the moment and giving the speaker one's full attention.

Shikha Pandey, a Mumbai-based mindfulness mindset coach, avers that active listening fosters empathy, strengthens relationships and creates an environment of respect and trust, thereby having profound effects on our brains and emotional well-being. As a human behavioural response, active listening by leaders makes their team members feel valued and act positively. One of the most important behavioural aspects of sustainable leadership is compassion. When we lack compassion, our strength becomes self-serving, fostering a sense of superiority and isolation. It limits us, as true power lies not in holding others down but in lifting them up. Cultivating compassion transforms one's inner strength into an external force that inspires and uplifts those around us. Strength alone imposes the burden of responsibility on the leader, whereas if coupled with compassion, it fosters a connection and shared accountability between the leader and the team. The strength of a compassionate leader empowers others, creating a ripple effect of growth and resilience that benefits everyone. True leadership isn't about standing alone—it's about standing along.

Convincing Authority

People with a higher intelligence quotient (IQ) are sure of their abilities and hence more likely to take calculated risks without the fear of losing. They make their presence felt in a positive manner during crisis situations, and are therefore more comfortable indulging in out-of-the-box thinking. Such people, sure of winning in their mind, can be said to possess

'convincing authority'. I believe that high IQ is mostly hidden or unknown even to the person concerned but emerges strongly in the face of a challenge. Realizing that 'from tiny acorns grow mighty oaks', a leader should be obligated to identify such members of the team and allow them space to grow. In such a situation, leaders need to use both their heart and brain for optimal use of all the human and non-human resources available to them. Planning involves the brain, while dealing with humans needs a heart approach. Leaders ought to be soft and subtle when interacting with humans, and strong and firm when planning, designing and executing projects.

One of the most evocative incidents I wish to recount here occurred in Kashmir in 2010, when major unrest followed the death of a seventeen-year-old boy, Tufail Mattoo, in police firing, which left around 117 people dead. When the protests were at their peak in September 2010, the Hurriyat Conference gave the call to march towards the security forces' camps in the Kashmir Valley. The army asked people to ignore the Hurriyat's call. Colonel Prashant Nikam, Bar to Sena Medal Gallantry, a Rajputana Rifles officer who had served with me in Manipur in 1997–99, was then posted as deputy sector commander of a Rashtriya Rifles sector deployed in North Kashmir. He called all the village elders, *maulvis* (religious preachers) and *sarpanches* (headmen), urging them to prevail upon the young boys to ignore the Hurriyat call. He also informed them that all the security forces' posts had been fitted with video cameras at the gate, which would capture the hooligans' faces, and that they could verify his statement by seeing the cameras fitted just outside the post. This polite conversation worked and

no protestors came near any post. I was posted to the same Rashtriya Rifles sector as commander in December 2010. When I was being briefed about the past events, I asked for more details about this particular event. Col Nikam came forward and told me that it was a proactive step to avoid any confrontation and collateral damage. The situation was thus handled sensibly by deploying convincing authority. I also imbibed this lesson of resolving potentially violent situations with dialogue instead of force, using it very effectively in all my future interactions with the locals.

Who Truly Owns Your Organization?

Ownership

The dictionary meaning of the word 'ownership' is 'the state, relation, or fact of being an owner, as also the rights or interests of an owner'. However, for leaders or the team, it goes beyond this definition, entailing that a leader or a team member should step up and 'take the responsibility for an idea or problem'. When I was the corps commander in Kashmir during 2019–20, Lieutenant Colonel Ratul Kapoor, a young energetic officer, was a colleague posted in the headquarters. We met a few times during professional and social functions. Thereafter, we remained in touch on social media, wishing each other on festivals and other social dates. After my retirement, and towards the end of 2024, I ordered a television through one of India's largest and most popular online shopping platforms. The delivery of the television was done on schedule but the installation was getting delayed beyond the promised timeline. I took up the matter with the online customer care department of the shopping platform. The routine promises of good services through unending

emails and messages continued for a few days without any positive outcome. After some days, when I got fed up, I posted about my unpleasant experience with this particular online shopping platform on my social media handle. Suddenly, the online platform's social media team got into the act, asking me to share the order details in their inbox. Despite my response containing all the details and the exchange of numerous messages over the next couple of days, nothing happened, adding to my frustration with their poor service.

Almost at the end of my patience, I received a WhatsApp message from Lieutenant Colonel Ratul Kapoor asking for the order details and volunteering to help resolve the issue. Thinking that he was trying to help through one of his contacts, I politely thanked him and told him not to bother. It was then that he informed me about his early retirement from the army, after which he had joined this online shopping platform at a particular position, which, however, did not involve dealing with sales or complaints. I again thanked him for his offer to help, telling him that the concerned department would do the needful. But I was both stunned and elated by his reply. He said, 'Sir, I have served in the army for more than twenty years. **The army has taught me to work for my organization as if I own that organization**, and now that I work for this organization, I will make sure it delivers to the customers' satisfaction. Although your issue is not within my job's charter, yet I am part of this organization and I must ensure that it lives up to its name and reputation. That's what the army has taught me and I carry my learning wherever I go.' This small but significant incident reinforced my conviction that the ethos of military leadership is as relevant in corporate businesses as it is in the military. If

Lieutenant Colonel Ratul Kapoor, as a veteran, can carry this ethos and values with him, corporate business houses would also do well to incorporate them in their working culture. As management schools repeatedly emphasize, we are always just one decision away from a totally different life, a decision that's difficult to take but easy to execute. Owning your organization is one such decision; take it today.

Belonging

As a corollary to ownership, belonging is another important aspect of a team game. Every team member must strive to belong to a team and contribute to it to the best of their ability. A saying in the army goes, 'We sail together, and we sink together.' If you belong to the team, you will make all efforts not to sink to ensure that everyone sails. I vividly remember watching the final FIFA World Cup match between France and Argentina in December 2022 at Qatar. Although Argentina won that match, I cannot forget the moment when the French President Emmanuel Macron went down to the ground and hugged France's forward Kylian Mbappe at the end of the game. Later, the President visited the players' locker room to console all of the French team, telling them how proud they had made their country feel. This one incident overshadowed Argentina's well-deserved victory. Although President Macron was not part of the French football team, he conveyed his sense of belonging to the team through his unparalleled gestures towards them. This is exactly how great leaders can motivate their teams by showing their sense of belonging to the latter. A leader with a sense of belonging would only be worrying about winning; while his competitors would always be worrying about the winner.

In the NDA, cadets are issued bicycles for commuting from one place to another. Technically, the bicycle belongs to the cadet for the three-year duration of his training in the academy, but actually it is the cadet who belongs to that bicycle because he has to carry his bicycle everywhere he goes. This rule contains a military training lesson. As revealed in an earlier chapter in this book, the Indian Army has the honour code of 'leaving no one behind, not even their dead'. The inculcation of this honour code in each cadet begins as early as the first term of the cadet's training at the NDA, where he is told never to leave his bicycle behind. This lesson learnt early in life later teaches a soldier never to leave his buddy or any other colleague behind, not even the mortal remains of those who went down fighting. And that is a steely display of the sense of belonging under extremely adverse circumstances.

Passion Versus Belonging

There is a subtle difference between a sense of belonging and being passionate about what you are doing. Passion implies a strong emotion, liking or desire for an object or devotion to perform some activity, whereas a sense of belonging is a psychological feeling of connectedness to a social, spatial, cultural, professional or other type of group or a community. Passion is a fundamental human emotion that dictates various mental, physical, social, economic and behavioural outcomes. Someone once asked me, 'Do people with the passion for a particular field make money in that field or do people who enter a field purely with the aim to make money do so?' My simple reply was, 'Passion can drive you but it is your aims and sense of belonging that will make you arrive at your destination.'

When I was a cadet in the NDA during the period 1980–82, the academy had a drill instructor named Subedar Darbara Singh from the Sikh Regiment. He was a tall, well-built JCO with a tremendous connect with the cadets, for whom he was a constant source of motivation, especially during the drill periods. Subedar Darbara Singh was promoted to the rank of subedar major in the middle of our training period at the academy. The NDA passing-out parade is held twice a year at the Arun Khetarpal Parade Ground in Khadakwasla, Pune, and it is a grand ceremonial spectacle that marks the culmination of a rigorous three-year-long training of cadets at the academy. The Drill Square is named after Second Lieutenant Arun Khetarpal, Param Vir Chakra (14 October 1950–16 December 1971), who made the supreme sacrifice during the 1971 Indo–Pak War at the young age of twenty-one years.

Participating in the parade is a matter of pride for every cadet, as it signifies their ability to become part of a new generation of warriors who would safeguard India's sovereignty and integrity. Before the commencement of the parade, all the cadets would line up inside the Quartermaster Fort just adjacent to the parade ground, smartly marching on to the Drill Square at the designated time. Subedar Major Darbara Singh would always address the cadets inside the Quartermaster Fort moments before they moved out for the parade. I can still hear his words thundering in my ears even after more than four decades, '*Yeh Drill Square sirf ek parade ground nahi hai, yeh ek mandir hai jahan par dharti maa ki seva karne wale sapoot paida hote hain aur aap woh sapoot ho. Yeh mandir aapka hai aur aap is mandir ke ho* (This Drill Square is not merely a parade ground, it is a temple where brave-hearts are born, who will serve the motherland, and

you are those warriors. This temple belongs to you and you belong to this temple).' This sense of 'belonging' drilled in the minds of young cadets by Subedar Major Darbara Singh is the lifetime lesson we learnt and have been implementing throughout our army lives. Second Lieutenant Arun Khetarpal, Param Vir Chakra, also 'belonged' to the same drill square that is now named after him. It is not without reason that the NDA is considered a 'cradle for military leadership' in India.

'Men Apart, Every Man an Emperor'

This motto of the Indian Army's Parachute Regiment Special Forces means that each and every soldier is a one-man strike force, even though they may be part of a larger, more indomitable group. Having the individual capacity and inherent belief to take ownership of any event or project is the most definitive attribute of adaptive leadership. The highly successful entrepreneur, speaker, investor and writer Tim Fargo wisely pointed out, **'Your friends will believe in your potential; your enemies will make you live up to it.'** Just like the ethos of the Special Forces, corporate employees must believe in themselves to achieve the individual targets assigned to them even though they may be part of a larger team. There are numerous extraordinary tales of ice-cold, steely nerves, raw courage and sacrifice among India's elite warriors, some well-known but most of them unknown.

India's Special Forces trace their origin to Meghdoot Force, an ad hoc commando unit organized by the legendary Major Megh Singh with the help of volunteers from various infantry units. This force conducted successful raids behind enemy lines during the 1965 Indo–Pak War, and was formally raised as 9 Para Commando in July 1966.

India's Special Forces have proved their mettle in the most challenging combat environments in Jammu and Kashmir and the north-eastern region over the last few decades by virtue of their ethos, commitment, esprit de corps and excellent junior leadership. This commitment and esprit de corps are echoed in the words of Major Sudhir Kumar Walia, Ashok Chakra (Posthumous), Sena Medal (Bar) of 9th Battalion The Parachute Regiment (Special Forces): 'I won't die in an accident or of any disease, I will go down in glory.' There is an unsaid belief in the military that when you see men falling from the sky, just bow down before them because they are going to rule the place from thereon—this analogy refers to the manner in which the Special Forces descend upon the enemy from the sky, the route usually taken by the gods. When employed as a force multiplier in any form of warfare, the Special Forces are akin to divine intervention.

I must make a special mention of my association with the Special Forces while operating in the icy heights of Sikkim and the jungles of Manipur, Lolab, Rajwar and Tral in Kashmir, and especially the Special Forces units under my command as the Chinar Corps commander in the Kashmir Valley during the most challenging periods of the post-Pulwama IED blast and the abrogation of Articles 370 and 35A of the Constitution on 5 August 2019. I have been singularly fortunate to have served with all the units of the Parachute Regiment, wherein I learnt a lot from the young officers, experienced JCOs and the full-of-*josh* (energy) and enthusiastic NCOs. I recall my bonding with Captain Vivek Singh Bhandral of 21 Para (SF), whose team was co-located within my post when I, as a major, was the Rashtriya Rifles

company commander in South Lolab during the intense terrorism days of 1999–2000. We operated together in the jungles of Lolab for many months, and though junior to me, he and his men taught me the art of lying doggo in ambush over seven to ten days at a stretch.

During one of the numerous occasions when we were lying in ambush together, waiting for the terrorists to make a movement on the fallen leaves, he told me to observe the surroundings and try to hear the rustle of their feet. When I could not see or hear anything, I told him that all I witnessed was absolute silence all around. His response was, **'Yes Sir, silence speaks and it speaks the loudest.'** Realizing that I was just nodding without understanding what he was saying, he explained that the entire jungle is littered with fallen dry leaves and anyone walking on them would make a noise, which is a signal that someone is approaching. Since at that time, none of our soldiers was moving and civilians never ventured into these thick forests, the breaking of silence would warn us about the incoming terrorists or a wild animal. I used this highly successful technique on a large scale subsequently when I was the Rashtriya Rifles sector commander in the neighbouring forests of Rajwar during the period 2010–12, with exemplary results.

Two years after our Lolab tenure, my association with Captain Bhandral continued when I returned to the Valley as commanding officer of an infantry battalion. He was now Major Vivek Bhandral, and I asked for him by name to be part of my battalion team for a highly sensitive special mission. Sadly, soon after, when he returned to his unit, I learnt about the news of this brave officer making the supreme sacrifice in a most daring act while fighting Pakistani terrorists in

the Kupwara sector in North Kashmir on 29 August 2002. People talk of Sir Basil Henry Liddell Hart (1895–1970), a British military strategist and historian, as the 'Captain who taught the Generals'. We had our own Captain Vivek Singh Bhandral, who taught the generals—a captain who was truly an emperor in his own right!

Silence Speaks the Loudest

I have seen people appreciating the work of their subordinates during special ceremonies by presenting them impressive individual mementoes or titles like 'Employee of the Month'. These presentations are all very good going by the phrase, 'Appreciate in public, scold in private'; but as a military leader who has to carry the team like an unshakable unit, this, at times, can foster feelings of unhealthy competition, or even jealousy among the team members. On the other hand, publicly rebuking a team member can also have an adverse effect on the morale of the team. If a child is lying to its parents, it's the parents' fault, as they did not give the child proper space to tell the truth. The child in this case would be unwilling to tell the truth if they are scared of punishment or of being judged, criticized, love withdrawal, sarcasm or contempt. I have learnt from experience that in any interaction with impressionable children or interns at work, silent admiration is the loudest soundless compliment. A silent nod of the head or a light pat on the shoulder works wonders, offering much more encouragement than loud appreciative speeches. Young, enthusiastic team members must also remember that initial acknowledgement of their efforts will always be laid-back and lethargic; but it's going to be a very definitive and prompt phenomenon when others will no longer be able to ignore their efforts and success. Further, if honed into a

relationship, this silence mutely conveys mutual admiration of each other's strengths and acceptance of weaknesses, which forms the crux of every close relationship. It is futile to force others to appreciate you; instead, one should win appreciation through one's actions. In a world full of options and priorities, let others decide their path; you choose yours. Other people's opinions should never be allowed to define an individual's worth.

Do People Leave Bad Jobs?

People do not give up bad jobs; they leave bad managers. Many business honchos complain of attrition among their trained employees. My argument in such a case is that if a trained and productive employee is leaving a company, and the management is feeling the pinch of losing that employee, the management needs to analyse the reasons for the loss of that worker. The reasons can vary from low salary, lack of work ethics, uncertain personal growth and an unhappy workplace, to name a few. However, the commonest reason for employees to switch companies, or 'job hopping' as it is also called, is bad bosses or bosses with a poor temperament.

Here again, it is important to reiterate the difference between a manager and a leader when it comes to dealing with humans. Immature managers instil fear, whereas leaders encourage growth, not only of the company as a whole but also of individual employees. We thus need more leaders and fewer managers in the higher positions of any organization. We need leaders who do not judge but build the morale of their team members, especially a youngster fresh out of college, who needs to be nurtured and provided a space to grow and evolve. It is such an environment of nurturing that leads to the evolution of leaders and great personalities, such as Nelson Mandela, Dhirubhai Ambani, Sachin Tendulkar and Sam Bahadur Manekshaw, to name just a few.

As far as employees are concerned, I would advise them to build their lives around their work, but never to give up 'living' in the process; because there's this whole life you may miss out on while working to build that very same life. Life's goals must therefore be interspersed with real 'life' that needs to be lived and enjoyed. Life can be equated to a nursery school race where you run with a marble in a spoon held in your mouth. If the marble falls, crossing the finish line first is a wasted effort. Similarly, in life, the marble can be likened to good health and personal relationships, where coming first in the race matters only if the marble is still in the spoon. Family, friends, books, coffee, a good laugh and great chilly or sunny weather are the best cures for life's challenges. So, get up and live life to the fullest without letting the marble fall from the spoon.

'Life should be great rather than long.'
—B.R. Ambedkar

8

Sustaining Passion and Balancing Emotions

यस्य कृत्यं न विघ्नन्ति शीतमुष्णं भयं रतिः ||
समृद्धिरसमृद्धिर्वा स वै राजर्षिः उच्यते ||

*'That person who can achieve things beyond the
limitations of external and internal circumstances,
whose judgements are not impaired by attachments, who
remains sane in prosperity or adversity is undoubtedly a
wise person capable of the position of power.'*

Sowing the Seeds of Passion

Passion is defined as an intense, deeply stirring emotion that compels action, fervour, ardour, enthusiasm or zeal. As a soldier, I have always believed in the adage that one must work today as if there's no tomorrow but was simultaneously also committed to working with such passion as if I was going to be crowned asking tomorrow.

Recently, while I was delivering a lecture titled 'What Drives a Soldier to Do What He Does', an elderly lady asked me, 'General, how strong a man do you think you are?'

My humble response was, **'Ma'am, I don't think of myself as being stronger than even your little grandchild, but my foes think that I am stronger than their gods.'**

Such words embody the passion that also fosters self-belief and self-confidence. Similarly, the passion of the defence forces is driven by the honour code of 'Naam, Namak, Nishan' and 'Wafadari, Imaandari, Zimmedari', which have been discussed in detail in the earlier chapters. However, in order to sustain such passion throughout a chequered career stretching across decades, soldiers need to select their battles wisely and be careful not to burn the candle at both ends, lest they fall short of wax during the darkest phase of the night that may lie ahead.

Zimmedari Drives Passion

It is not necessary to wear the uniform to be a responsible citizen. In normal circumstances, a person with passion would be expected to perform his job with a sense of responsibility (zimmedari). In the military, on the other hand, it is zimmedari that will drive the individual to perform his duty with passion (*shiddat se*).

This thought reminds me of an incident dating as far back as 1990, when as a young captain, I was posted as an instructor at the Infantry School in Mhow. A havildar from my unit, Hazari Singh, was also posted as an NCO instructor along with me. Hazari Singh, who subsequently retired as a subedar, was not only an excellent instructor but also a daredevil soldier, who had been part of my team in the battalion during several operations. He lived with his family in the government family quarters allotted to staff within the Infantry School complex, which was bifurcated by the Agra–Mumbai national highway that passed right through the centre of the complex. The national highway witnessed heavy truck traffic throughout the day and night,

posing a special risk for soldiers and their families whose quarters were right next to the highway. And sure enough, the potential risk turned into reality when one day Havildar Hazari Singh's little son, who was playing near his home, was run over by a speeding truck as he tried to cross the road to retrieve his cricket ball that had rolled to the other side. The child was immediately taken to the military hospital and my wife Nita and I rushed there as soon as we heard the news.

When I reached the hospital, coming face to face with the shattered soldier standing outside the operation theatre where his child was battling for life was, without doubt, one of the most challenging moments in my military career. My wife went and sat next to his wife on a bench a little distance away. As I greeted her with a *'Namaskar'*, her woeful eyes pierced my soul, and I could not summon any response to her tearful plea, *'Sahib, mere bachche ko bacha lo* (Sir, please save my child).' Then she turned to her husband, silently asking if his officer could somehow work a miracle and prevent the looming tragedy. As I proceeded towards the operation theatre, I could feel within myself that look from the mother conveying a hundred feelings and asking a thousand questions from the officer of her husband. As I traversed the short distance but long journey through the corridor, my shoulders were weighed down by a heavy responsibility that I was loath to deliver. Havildar Hazari Singh, positioned at the door of the operation theatre, saluted me with the same soldierly pride and *fauji dastoor* (military traditions) but a demeanour that was clearly overshadowed by a father's emotions. Soon thereafter, the doctors called me inside to share the unfortunate news that their efforts had been in vain, and it was now left to me to inform the parents about their child's death.

A commander in the army is confronted with numerous challenges in the course of his career but one of his most difficult tasks is to lay a wreath on the mortal remains of his comrade and offer him a salute for one last time, and even worse, call the next of kin to inform them about the death of their loved one. This situation was even more delicate, as I had to convey this information to the parents in person. I was only twenty-eight years old and not yet a father myself at that time, but was faced with this zimmedari as the officer around. Although a few other officers and JCOs had arrived at the hospital, some of them senior to me in rank and age, the responsibility of delivering the bad news remained with me as Havildar Hazari Singh belonged to my paltan; and each member of your paltan is your family.

I first conveyed the news to my wife Nita, who herself was just twenty-three years old, speaking to her in English so that she could muster her courage to be brave and take care of the child's mother. Then, I walked towards Hazari Singh and placed my hand on his shoulder. Realizing that something was amiss, his wife started crying out loudly. The havildar maintained a stoic silence, then said softly, '*Sahib, bachche ko kisi bade hospital mein le jaate hain* (Sir, we should take the child to a bigger hospital)?' Not going into what happened thereafter, all I can say is that a soldier attains maturity not with age but with the sense of responsibility that his position places upon him, irrespective of age or lack of training to deal with such poignant episodes. Even as these kinds of incidents occurring in non-combat situations test a soldier's emotional strength, what happens in the battlefield or combat zone is an even more challenging experience.

Nita accompanied the child's mother to their house, consoling her throughout without losing her own

composure. However, when we returned home later in the evening, Nita could not control her emotions any longer and broke down. Although such situations may also occur in a civilian's life, military wives have to learn to deal with them on a regular basis, without flinching or losing control. The mental and emotional transition that a young bride goes through as she becomes the wife of an army man is in itself one of the toughest lessons of life.

The Inherent Zimmedari of a 'Memsaab'

The term 'Memsaab' or 'Memsahib' signifies much more than the corresponding title of 'Ma'am' in a civilian or corporate environment, where the privileges are often outweighed by obligations. The word 'Memsahib', which has a genesis in the colonial era, is a combination of the English word 'Madam or Ma'am' and the Hindi and Urdu word 'Sahib'. It was used to address ladies in a position of authority or the wives of the English officials during the British rule. Although the British left India in 1947, the legacy of this term continues till date, with the wives of senior government officers as well as officers and JCOs in the defence forces still being endowed with this title.

I happened to meet Jyoti Barmola Mamgain, a prolific speaker, author and proud army wife, at a literary event in Chandigarh in February 2025. She was attending the event as the author of her popular book *Drills, Thrills and Spills: An Army Wife's Tales*. Since I had read her book, an enthralling account of the life of an army officer's wife or Memsahib, I decided to discuss with her the crucial issue of the responsibilities of an army officer's wife vis-à-vis the title of Memsahib bestowed upon her by her husband's profession. Below, I reproduce Jyoti Barmola Mamgain's account of her role as Memsahib, in her own words:

Fifteen years ago, living in Delhi, I found myself immersed in a fast-paced urban lifestyle, where the rhythm of the city became my own. My regular day began with a rush of energy, grabbing a half-baked toast that almost flew out of the oven as I hurried to get ready for work. The day continued with high-stakes client meetings where expectations were sky-high. I spent my time grappling with designs, applying all my marketing expertise to seal the deal and establish my newly formed company. And often, after work, I caught up with friends at trendy coffee shops or enjoyed home dinners with food delivered from fancy restaurants. Evenings were spent watching favourite movies on TV (OTT had yet to make its mark). And to top it all, the handsome payments from my clients made me feel like I had it all, especially at 25, in a city like Delhi.

Little did I know that one day I would meet a man who would completely pull me out of the carefully curated, fast-paced life I had built in the modern metro city and take me on a journey through the adventurous, engaging, evolving, and so fulfilling life of an Indian Army wife. From the first day itself it felt almost like stepping into a magical world, much like Alice entering Wonderland — where the way of living was completely different but so much more wholesome. As I wrote in my book *Drills, Thrills and Spills: An Army Wife's Tales*, it captures those transformative days and through delightful vignettes I celebrate the whole experience of being the better half of the man in uniform.

I have been an Army wife for almost 15 years now, and when I look back, I realize how beautifully and subtly this organization has shaped and evolved me as an individual. The gradual transformation from being a regular working girl in a metro to becoming an accomplished Army wife, carrying the responsibility of almost 200 families—and more—for their health, happiness, and overall well-being, has been a process that was both smooth and enriching. I often find myself pondering this and thinking, 'Isn't it magical how, by the virtue of our husbands donning the uniform, we as wives start feeling such a deep connection to this organization and want to contribute our best to it? Isn't it magical how, without any monetary gain, sacrificing certain comforts, and despite living on modest salaries, we craft a life that the world admires? What is this magic that holds us so tightly, making one family's pain feel like another family's agony? Isn't this truly magical?' There's a profound sense of belonging, a bond forged not by blood, but by shared experiences, sacrifices, and a commitment to something far greater than ourselves. We carry the weight of each other's struggles, celebrate each other's victories, and build a community that thrives on selflessness and resilience. And in this journey, we realize that what may seem like simple acts of kindness, loyalty, and support are, in fact, the threads that weave a stronger, united force—one that can weather any storm. I conclude this is truly magical.

Now, when I look back, I see so many incidents that I recognize as opportunities unique to an Army wife. These moments, though small at the time, gradually accumulate and shape you into the proud Indian Army wife you become. One such early encounter happened when I was a young bride. Like any other newlywed, full of childlike innocence, I was caught up in setting up my new home, wearing bright clothes, primarily sarees (an Indian garment for women), posting pictures with

my dapper husband and flaunting them before friends, while also experimenting in the kitchen to impress him. I was happily busy in my modest Fauji (soldier) home, like any new bride, adjusting to the new found role. It was a time of innocence and it was a time when I wasn't fully aware of the responsibilities that came with being an Army wife—or as we are more popularly known, a 'Memsahib'.

My husband was the company commander at that time, and he had explained to me a bit about being responsible for the families under his command. I had attended a welfare meet once at the battalion, and that was when I first learnt about house visits and started connecting with the families (soldiers' wives are called families in the Army irrespective of them being a newly married bride or an elderly lady with children) in our company. The sense of love, compassion, and inclusivity resonated with me from day one, even before I understood its technicalities.

At that time, my man in uniform was a Major Sahib, and those days, he was away on a field-firing exercise with his paltan (battalion) somewhere on the Western front. While he was away, I realised that the early days of separation were challenging but also full of opportunities to learn— making friends, learning to tie a saree and baking (early trials and tactical errors of almost every Army wife), while observing and slowly adapting to my new world.

One such afternoon, I received a call from the Unit Nursing Assistant (NA), who informed me about a family—a jawan's wife—who had been admitted to the Military Hospital (MH) the previous night. She had

been experiencing intense pain and skin eruptions. That call was a turning point, one of many, that would teach me the depth of responsibility and empathy required in this life.

When the NA called me to inform me about this particular family, I instantly knew the background, thanks to the welfare meets and house visits where I had found my footing. The jawan's wife was in her ninth month of pregnancy, expecting delivery within a few weeks. When I had met her during a house visit, she had told me, '*Memsahib, aap naye aaye ho, na, meri delivery bhi ab hone wali hai*' (You are new here, and I am also about to have a new member in my family). I had joked with her, realizing that I had no experience of motherhood or understanding what she was going through. '*Darr to nahin lag raha? Mujhe toh bahut lagta hai!*' (Are you feeling scared? I would feel really afraid if I were in your place). To which she replied, '**Memsahib, aapko darr kaise lag sakta hai, aap toh humare Memsahib ho!** (How can you feel afraid, you are our Memsahib).' I remembered those words for a long time—'*Aapko darr kaise lag sakta hai, aap toh humare Memsahib ho.*' They echoed in my mind, making me realize the immense trust placed in me. In that simple remark, I understood that being a Memsahib wasn't about my own fears or limitations anymore; it was about embodying strength and compassion for others.

When the NA called to tell me that the same lady had been admitted to the Military Hospital, I knew I had to act. Her husband had gone for a military exercise with my husband and almost the entire paltan was out, and she was all alone. I quickly changed into a suit, draped

my dupatta (a woman's head scarf, worn typically in North India), and rushed to the MH, understanding the seriousness of the situation.

Upon entering the hospital, the gynaecologist met me in her office. She spoke in a sombre tone and told me that the soldier's wife had lost her baby—sadly, the umbilical cord had gotten tangled around the neck, and the baby had died in the womb two days ago. The infection had spread to her uterus, and surgery was needed immediately for her survival. The problem was that the young expectant mother was refusing to believe it and would not allow anyone to touch her.

I was quiet, almost numb hearing this. I wasn't a mother myself, I never knew how it feels but then I was a woman, I felt a pricking pain in the heart, it almost brought tears to my eyes and I felt so weak, almost broken.

The gynaecologist urged me to speak with her and convince her to agree to the surgery, as it was now a matter of life and death. She further added that because it has been more than 48 hours that a dead baby was in the womb, the harmful fluids had spread in the body and it will be a complicated surgery. The gynaecologist handed me some papers to sign as a witness once she agreed to the procedure. The papers stated in intricate medical language about the complications involved and I had to sign them as no relatives were present. I had to not only take that crucial decision on her family's behalf but also make her agree. I still remember the chill that ran down my spine as I held those papers. My hand trembled as I signed, and I took a sip of water, trying to steady myself.

The gynecologist uttered, 'Ma'am, she is from your husband's company. You have to make her agree, she is not letting us touch her, it is dangerous for her, she has to agree.'

Merely in my mid-twenties myself and with no experience of handling such a situation, deep down I was nervous and equally scared, but the only choice I had was to act. I stood up, took a deep breath, and walked toward the family ward. I saw her lying on the bed, looking sad and alone. When she saw me enter, she rose with difficulty, her ninth-month pregnancy weighing heavily on her. Her eyes locked with mine, and she began to howl, howl in pain, in agony, in anger. She clung to me, burying her face in my body, her warmth and wet eyes telling me everything. She held me tightly, crying uncontrollably. That moment her pain became my pain. She was a mother who had nurtured a life inside her for nine long months, and now it was gone. What pain can be greater than this?

'*Main apna bachcha nahin dungi, ye log jhoot bol rahe hain, Memsahib, aap baat karo, mera bachcha theek hai* (I will not let them take away my baby, these people are lying. Please tell them that my baby is fine).'

I held her tightly, my heart touching hers, and we communicated through the silence, through our shared pain. What words would suffice? Which statement would console her? I knew at that moment nothing would work, but just being there with her in her pain, in her sorrow.

We remained like that for a long while, me wiping her tears silently, she asking me constantly why this was happening to her and I had no answers to that. I just

stayed strong; I had to, for her sake, the only option I had in my hand in that moment.

Finally, I managed to calm her down, spoke to her, consoled her and after a while, she finally heard her Memsahib. I still don't know from where those words came in me, I spoke with conviction, certainty and compassion; I spoke for what had to be done now for her good. She saw directly into my eyes that pain-struck look almost gazed my soul, I connected with her, I looked back at her with hope, with assurance while my words tried to uplift her.

That moment was unexplainable. I don't know where that Shakti (strength) was coming in me, but my words seemed to transcend into her. She finally agreed, trusting what I told her, what her Memsahib had said. With a final, heart-breaking look, she said, '*Theek hai Memsahib, jaise aap ko theek lage* (Okay, Memsahib, whatever you think is right)', and she nodded faintly. I signed the papers, and later that day, she underwent the surgery. That night, I couldn't sleep. Her screams echoed in my mind, and the trembling touch of her body, her bloodshot eyes and her screams haunted me. But knowing that I had helped her make the right decision gave me a strange sense of peace. Following a successful surgery, she is now a proud mother of two healthy children.

But that fateful day, I realized something profound: **Being called the 'Memsahib' was not just a title; it was a bond, a responsibility, a moral obligation, and above all an honour code to live by.** It is a responsibility that carried duties, expectations, and a deep connection to the system. It meant immersing yourself in the lives

of others, understanding their struggles, and offering compassion when they need it most.

That day, I truly became the Memsahib, I understood it more deeply and now after almost more than 15 years as an Army wife, I realized how beautifully it has helped me evolve as a person. It has enriched me as an individual, strengthened my character, and transcended me into a better human being - someone who can feel, love and give back in so many ways. After all, isn't that what life is all about?

Passion Versus Obsession

In the context of these incidents exemplifying the zimmedari displayed by army wives, I would like to bring the concept of 'disrupters' into the discourse, and suggest that *while the diligent folks exhibit passion, the disrupters work with obsession!* And I daresay that more than passion, military wives have the obsession that translates barren fields of wheat into a plentiful harvest.

When the disrupters enter the arena, the men get separated from the boys (this statement is suggestive and gender-neutral). I am often asked how army men remain motivated, not just for a day or a week or a month, but for their entire lifetime. There are three simple but unique traits that fuel a soldier's motivation levels not only during the length of their service but also post their retirement. These are discussed in detail below.

Confidence in the Weapon: A soldier has absolute confidence that the weapon they have been entrusted with is superior to that wielded by a terrorist or the enemy, and that it will not let them down at a crucial moment during a firefight, which is not only the main source of their motivation under any adverse situation, but also keeps alive their will to fight, come what may. In a corporate scenario, this can be equated to an employee's confidence that the product being offered by their company is superior to that of the competitor, which motivates them to market the product with vigour and gumption.

Confidence in the Buddy: The second important factor that motivates a soldier during both war and peacetime is their confidence in their buddy, and the conviction that their buddy will never abandon them. This confidence in an absolutely dependable colleague standing shoulder to shoulder with them in the battle fosters an unmatched willpower in the soldier to perform their duty without any inhibition. In a corporate scenario, this implies that the motivation of each member of a team is driven by a confidence in both their individual abilities and the collective efficiency of the entire team.

Confidence in the Commander: Last but not least, the most critical factor that nurtures motivation in a soldier is their confidence in their commander, and the belief that the commander's plans and strategy would ensure not only the success of the team's operation but also the safety and well-being of the team members. It is this confidence that turns a commander or a CEO or a director or a boss into a leader. A leader would do well to always remember Lao Tzu's quote, 'Do the difficult things while they are easy and do the great things while they are small. A journey of a thousand miles must begin with a single step.'

'Dekh lena, ho sake jaise kar lena' Versus Determination and Resolve

How many times have we heard an ostensibly liberal but puny instruction, *'Dekh lena, ho sake jaise kar lena* (See and somehow manage to do it)' from our bosses or parents. In contrast, a military commander always issues crystal-clear instructions, be they written or verbal. As reiterated in an earlier chapter, *'Nischay kar apni jeet karun* (My determination will make me triumphant)' is a phrase extracted from *'Deh Shiva Bar Mohe Eha'*, a Sikh prayer and the Sikh national anthem. It is a prayer to the Almighty, requesting for the ability to do good deeds, to be fearless in combat and to be victorious. A commander needs to conceptualize his vision, plan his mission and chart out action in a very lucid and clinical manner, right up to the desired end state. Following are the main non-negotiable elements of this strategy:

Vision: As one of the core attributes of leadership, having a clear vision will lay the foundation for an inspiring journey, guiding the team members carefully but surely towards their target and to a desired end state.

Identification and Selection of an Aim: The leader must set an indomitable aim for the team, which cannot be diluted or neutralized by any apprehensions or doubts among the team members. The lack of a well-defined objective or mandate foments ambiguity, creating the situation of a 'dekh lena, ho sake jaise kar lena' situation, which is a recipe for disaster.

Sustenance of the Aim and Maintenance of Momentum: The journey will be peppered with ups and downs but that should not deter a leader and his team from attaining their objective. It is therefore imperative to consistently sustain the momentum towards achieving the aim.

Clear and Sharp Orders and Instructions: During our training in the Indian Military Academy, we were taught how to deliver clear and unambiguous verbal orders to our team. I still remember the lines from the training pamphlet that the orders must be given as orders and obeyed as such. And these orders had to be issued in a very calm, clear and concise manner. A senior may pass a direction or an instruction during a casual discussion with the team over a cup of coffee or an informal conversation during the games period; but in the end, for the subordinate, an order is an order and should be obeyed as such.

Maintaining Focus: The leader and the team must also maintain their focus on achieving their aim through single-minded dedication and commitment. In the Indian epic Mahabharata, Guru Dronacharya asks all the five Pandava brothers to aim their arrows at the eye of the rotating fish suspended in the air above by looking down at its reflection in the water placed on the ground. As the brothers came up to take their respective aims, Dronacharya asked each one of them what they saw. Four of them barring Arjuna replied that they saw the fish, trees, the sky and various other objects in the vicinity of the rotating fish. It was only Arjuna who replied, 'I only see the eye of the fish.' The skilled archer that Arjuna was, his single-minded focus on the objective before him allowed him to successfully aim at the eye of the fish. This parable also underscores the virtue of concentrating on one task at a time rather than multitasking, which may dilute focus, thereby impacting crucial tasks that need to be prioritized over

others. Some people will argue that multitasking is a virtue. It is important to understand that focus while multitasking is a paradox. Tying shoelaces while talking on the phone is okay if we call it multitasking but important jobs need to be prioritized and handled with 100 per cent focus at a time.

Catering for 'Fog of War' and 'Noise': The term 'fog of war' is used in the military to describe uncertainties in military situations or voids in intelligence about the enemy that need to be taken into account during strategizing and planning. Similarly, the term 'noise' refers to unnecessary clutter that lacks any intelligence value. Since every operation is bound to be affected by 'noise' and 'fog of war', a leader must invariably cater for such uncertainties or unnecessary information in his plans and lay out ways to tackle them. An example I would like to cite here to show how fog and noise can disrupt focus pertains to an incident that occurred during a football match between the Chelsea and Charlton football clubs at the Stamford Bridge Stadium in London in December 1937. It was a typical English winter evening with an overcast sky and dense fog. As the 'fog' reduced visibility, the game was halted after about an hour. However, Charlton's goalkeeper Sam Bartram could not hear the referee's whistle due to the noise from the crowd, and unaware that play had been abandoned, he kept on guarding the goal for at least fifteen minutes after the game had been stopped. Eventually, the stadium police near the goalpost had to intimate him about the suspension of the match. Sam Bartram's reaction was, 'How sad that my friends forgot me when I was guarding their gate.'

Achieving the End State: Last but not least, achieving the end state provides the finality to the aim.

Balancing Emotions with Operational Imperatives

The famous words of Ralph Waldo Emerson, 'Do not go where the path may lead, go instead where there is no path and leave a trail', underlie the trajectory of a leader's journey. These words imply that a leader must be daring enough to tread into uncharted territory where few have dared to go in the past. A commander in the army has to factor in various intricacies that impact military operations and their fallout in his plans. This necessitates intimate knowledge of variable factors, such as the nature of the enemy, the terrain and weather conditions. In the same context, junior leaders often position themselves at the ground level in close proximity to the soldiers. This move is a psychological response to a situation wherein a soldier's behaviour may be coloured by human emotions like sadness, happiness, fear and anger, which, coupled with exigent operational and environmental factors, may hamper logical thinking. The leader thus needs to prioritize the emotions of his team members even during the most critical juncture in a battle or combat situation. He has to master the art of coalescing commitment to duty with human emotions, woven together with utmost military precision and laid out in an easily comprehensible form for the benefit of the team members. As William Shakespeare very famously said, 'It is not in the stars to hold our destiny but in ourselves.' The significance of emotions in a soldier's life is highlighted by Captain R. Subramanian, Kirti Chakra (Posthumous), a brave-heart of 1 Para (SF), who made the supreme sacrifice in Haphruda Forest in North Kashmir in June 2000. This was also the area where I operated as a young captain in 1989–90, and later commanded a Rashtriya Rifles Sector during 2010–12. Captain Subramanian's words still

ring in my ears, 'You have never lived until you have almost died, and for those who choose to fight, life has a special flavour, the protected will never know!'

Empathy Towards the Enemy

The honour codes followed by the Indian Army in any battle have been described in a previous chapter. One of these codes is 'Respect for the Dead Enemy', who too goes all out to defend their country, even laying down their life for their country. Recall here the videos providing an account of the Kargil War, wherein Pakistan refused to take back the mortal remains of their dead soldiers even when the Indian side offered to hand them over to Pakistan. Disowned by their own country, these dead Pakistani soldiers were accorded a decent burial on the Indian side of the battlefield by Lieutenant Colonel (later Lieutenant General) Yogesh Kumar Joshi, the then officiating commanding officer of the 13 Jammu and Kashmir Rifles Regiment. This incident emphasizes the value of a humanitarian and empathetic approach towards the enemy, no matter how hard-fought or acrimonious the battle with the same enemy may have been.[7]

Major General Naveen Kumar Airy, my NDA course-mate and a dear friend, narrated a lesser-known incident from the 1971 Indo–Pak War wherein his father, Lieutenant Colonel (later Lieutenant General) Ved Prakash Airy was commanding the 3 Grenadiers in the Shakargarh sector of Western Punjab. It is the same sector where Second Lieutenant Arun Khetarpal earned his Param Vir Chakra

---

[7] Many such incidents pertaining to the Kargil War have been narrated in detail by Lieutenant General Y.K. Joshi in his recently published book, *Who Dares Wins* (Gurugram: Penguin Veer, 2024).

in the famous battle of Basantar in an assault on enemy positions in his tank to support the 3 Grenadiers.

The Indian soldiers displayed nerves of steel and unmatched courage in the battle of Basantar, one of the bloodiest encounters in the 1971 war. During one such battle for Barapind village in the Jarpal sub-sector on 17 December 1971, Lieutenant Colonel Airy's battalion was facing the 35 Frontier Force (FF) Regiment of the Pakistan Army. The 3 Grenadiers had captured the enemy positions of Jarpal and Lohal. The 35 FF commanded by Lieutenant Colonel Muhammad Akram Raja of the Pakistan Army was tasked to counter-attack Jarpal to win it back from the Indians. Personally leading the counter-attack, Lt Col Raja was killed in the first wave of the attack, as he was shot in the face and chest in a hail of machine gun fire, barely 50 metres from the forward Indian defences, with his hands frozen on his carbine. The Pakistan Army launched seven fierce counter-attacks in one night to recapture their positions but without success.

After the ceasefire, on the morning of 18 December 1971, both sides started identifying and retrieving the bodies of their dead soldiers. A young captain from 35 FF identified the body of his CO, Lieutenant Colonel Muhammad Akram Raja in Jarpal village. Lieutenant Colonel Airy ordered the body of the CO to be placed in a casket and handed over to the Pakistan Army with full military honours. Lieutenant Colonel Airy also sent a handwritten citation dated 18 December 1971 stating that Lieutenant Colonel Raja had 'died a real soldier's death' and 'our hats off to him'. This citation, written on the battlefield on the log book page, was handed over to the brigade commander of the Pakistan Army along with the body. Later Col Raja's watch and one epaulette of the ranks were also placed in a small silver box and handed over to the Pakistan Army during a flag meeting, to be handed over to Raja's wife. The other epaulette of the rank of Lieutenant Colonel Raja's uniform is still displayed in the 3 Grenadiers Officers' Mess.

Based on the note written by Lieutenant Colonel Airy, Lieutenant Colonel Muhammad Akram Raja was honoured with the Hilal-i-Jur'at award, Pakistan's second highest military honour. Lieutenant Colonel Airy was also awarded the Maha Vir Chakra, the second highest military decoration of India. Major Hoshiar Singh of 3 Grenadiers, whose company repulsed seven enemy counter-attacks in one night, was awarded the Param Vir Chakra, India's highest military decoration awarded for displaying supreme valour or self-sacrifice in the presence of the enemy. As per the Regimental traditions, the 3 Grenadiers celebrate their victory at Jarpal as 'Jarpal Day' every year since 1971.

Thirty-five years later, in 2006, the 3 Grenadiers, now being commanded by Colonel Ashutosh Kale, were deployed in Eritrea–Ethiopia as part of the United Nations Peacekeeping mission. A Pakistani Army officer, Major Yusuf Jamal from 35 FF, the battalion that had fought the 3 Grenadiers at Jarpal in 1971, was also posted as a UN observer in the same mission. Colonel Ashutosh Kale invited the Pakistani officer to the unit on the occasion of Jarpal Day celebrations, who graciously agreed to attend after some initial recalcitrance. Major Jamal also attended the subsequent *puja* (prayers) at the temple. During a wreath-laying ceremony to honour the dead at a makeshift war memorial, Colonel Kale invited Major Yusuf Jamal to march with him and lay the wreaths jointly. Signifying the most invaluable traditions of the Indian Army, including the honour code of respecting the dead enemy, the wreaths that day were laid for every brave-heart who fought and died in the battle of Jarpal, irrespective of the army he belonged to.

Subsequently, the portraits of Colonel V.P. Airy and Colonel Muhammad Akram Raja were exchanged, and today these paintings proudly adorn the walls of the Officers' Messes of both battalions. Much later, Colonel S.S. Cheema, the second frontline company commander of 3 Grenadiers during the battle of Jarpal, spoke at length to Major Yusuf. It turned out that Colonel Cheema's ancestral village in Pakistan was also the village of Yusuf Jamal's mother. A poignant reminder of the truth that wars are often fought to protect territories but their fallout does not respect boundaries!

This story was published in the Indian media—in *The Hindu* on 4 January 2021 and ThePrint on 20 March 2021. It was also covered in the Pakistani media, wherein Major Ghiasuddin Babar of 40 Punjab Regiment of the Pakistan Army narrated an account of this battle, mentioning the act of Lieutenant Colonel V.P. Airy in an article titled, 'Major Ghiasud Din Babar of 40 Punjab Recollects the Bara Pind Jarpal Fiasco of 1971', authored by Agha H. Amin. This article was published in a Pakistani magazine, *India Pakistan Afghanistan Military Review*, under the title 'An Infantry Direct Participant Remembers Barapind Battles', in its January 2018 issue. I quote from the article in the Pakistani magazine below:

This great Commanding Officer embraced martyrdom along with three officers, a junior commissioned officer (JCO) and 53 non-commissioned officers (NCOs) & Sepoys. Bengali officers of 35 FF also fought gallantly alongside their West Pakistani brethren, Lt Shahid Ullah from East Pakistan embraced Shahadat. These great heroes like Lt Col Raja Muhammad Akram Shaheed HJ and many others like him, are paid homage and respects even by the enemy for their gallant actions. Jarpal was held by 3 Grenadiers once 35 FF launched counter attack. Commanding Officer of 3 Grenadiers Lt Col V P Airy had written citation for the CO 35 FF paying him rich tributes for his bold action and bravery and had recommended him for a gallantry award. Few words of the citation are quoted here: 'We had recovered the body on 18th Dec 71 . . . we found both his arms frozen after death in the position in which he was holding his sten gun, which indicates his determination to get ahead. Col Muhammad Akram Raja displayed courage, determination and personal bravery of the highest order in keeping with the tradition of the soldiers. The heroic deed of Lt Col Raja should not go unnoticed.' After falling down of the brave Commanding Officer along with the two leading Company Commanders and number of men, attack could not progress any further. However, their brave and resilient forward observation officer (FOO) Captain Nur ul Hassan took on himself the responsibility to control and stabilize the situation by bringing effective artillery fire on enemy positions and with great determination and resolve, he was able to extricate rest of the troops under intense enemy tank and small arms fire. For boldness, courage and keeping his wits about under heavy odds, to retrieve attacking force in a precarious situation and re-assemble the assaulting troops, Captain Nur ul Hassan was awarded Sitara-e-Jurrat. For highest courage and bravery in the face of enemy, C & D Company Commanders Major Zulfiqar Ahmed Shaheed and Major Pervez Farooq Shaheed were also recommended for Sitara-e-Jurrat. Later on, Major Abdul Rehman of 40 Punjab on the

orders of Brigade Commander carried out evacuation of casualties by making a lane in the minefield.

Displaying extraordinary courage and exemplary leadership in beating back repeated counter attacks by Pakistani forces, Major Hoshiar Singh of 3 Grenadiers was awarded highest gallantry award of Indian Army; Param Vir Chakra making him the second recipient of PVC of Indian 47 Brigade in just two days.

The following picture depicts the citation (note) written by Lieutenant Colonel V.P. Airy.

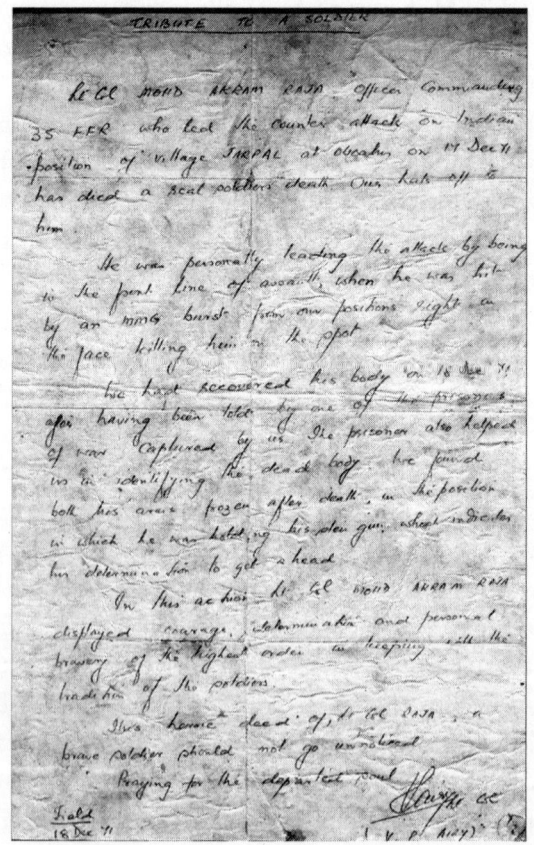

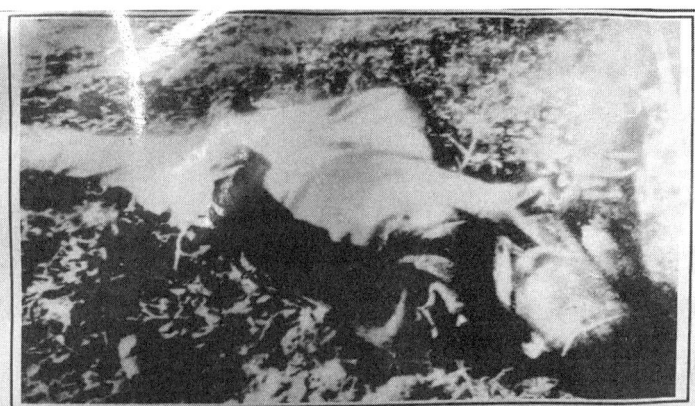

DEAD BODY OF LT COL MOHD AKRAM RAZA RECOVERED BY 3 GRENADIERS

TRIBUTE TO A SOLDIER

Lt Col MOHD AKRAM RAJA, Officer Commanding 35 FFR, who led the counter attack on Indian position of village JARPAL at 0400 hrs on 17 Dec 71, had died a real soldiers death. Our hats off to him.

He was personally leading the attack by being in the front line of assault, when he was hit by an MMG burst from our position right on the face killing him on the spot.

We had recovered his body on 17 Dec 71 after having been told by one of the prisoners of war captured by us. The prisoner also helped us in identifying the dead body. We found both his arms frozen after death in the position in which he was holding his sten gun, which indicates his determination to get ahead.

In this action Lt Col MOHD AKRAM RAJA displayed courage, determination and personal bravery of the highest order in keeping with the traditions of the soldiers.

This heroic deed of Lt Col RAJA, a brave soldier, should not go unnoticed.

Praying for the departed soul.

Field

18 Dec 71

Airy

Lt Col VP Airy

CITATION OF LT COL MOHD AKRAM RAZA, THE CO OF 35 FRONTIER FORCE WRITTEN BY LT COL VP AIRY, CO 3 GRENADIERS BASED ON WHICH HE WAS AWARDED HILAL-E-ZURRAT PAK EQUIVALENT OF MVC

While Lieutenant Colonel V.P. Airy, Maha Vir Chakra, rose to the rank of lieutenant general in the Indian Army, his two sons also joined the Grenadiers Regiment, retiring at the rank of major general. Interestingly, when I was posted as an instructor at the Infantry School Mhow as a captain, Lieutenant General V.P. Airy was the director general military training, overseeing the functioning of all the training institutions in the Indian Army, including the Infantry School. Once, when Lieutenant General Airy was on an official visit to the Infantry School for an inspection, I was detailed with him to carry out liaison officer duties. I received him at the Indore airport and escorted him to Mhow during very heavy rain. The Infantry School commandant received the lieutenant general in the guest room and left after a brief discussion. When Lieutenant General Airy entered his room, he saw two bowls of dry fruits on the table and quipped, 'When I was young and could eat them, no one offered me these; and now that I am growing old, I get these everywhere I go.' He emptied both the bowls filled with almonds and cashews in my pockets and said, 'Son, it's your age to eat them, enjoy.' I will always remember this act, embodying empathy and kindness from a senior for a junior colleague, who could offer little in return. Here I leave the readers with a quote.

'A great man is always willing to be little!'
—Ralph Waldo Emerson

9

Strong Families Help Build Strong Leaders

*'To support mother and father, to cherish wife and child,
and to have a simple livelihood; this is good luck.'*
—Buddha

Strong Families Raise Brave Soldiers

Family: As the Army Defines It

A family is defined as a basic unit or group comprising a few people related by birth, marriage or adoption, who live together. Needless to say that pets are an integral part of a family.

All members of a family may also have a common lineage by virtue of being descendants of a common ancestor. In the military, however, the definition of 'family' has many more implications. For instance, in a battalion or the paltan, the battalion itself is considered as a family with the commanding officer (CO) being the head of the family. Every member of the paltan, that is, serving officers, JCOs, soldiers, the veterans and their individual families (as defined above) are an integral part of the larger family of the battalion where everyone is always available to help each other in the time of need. In this way, the army as a whole can be seen as one big family.

Why is the paltan like a soldier's family in addition to his own family back home? When a young soldier of eighteen or a young officer of twenty-one years joins the paltan as a greenhorn, they hardly have any idea about life in the military, with their knowledge being limited to only what they read about the army in pamphlets or what they learn about it at the training centre or the pre-commission training academies. That knowledge is just the tip of the iceberg with regard to the vast spectrum of military activities either in peacetime or on the battlefield. Gradually, these youngsters' minds are moulded by on the job training in the paltan along with guidance from the seniors, peers and juniors alike. Every member of the paltan thus contributes in honing them into lean, mean fighting machines. Here, they jointly celebrate moments of happiness and share moments of grief. This relationship gains so much strength over years of training and togetherness that a soldier or an officer is willing to lay down his life for the paltan's izzat.

Interestingly, the term 'family' has another definition in the Indian Army. In a battalion, the wife of a soldier is also referred to as 'family', even when the couple are newly married and may not have any children or other relatives staying with them. This concept was very poignantly explained by Dr Rajni Lamba, a *fauji* daughter and friend from Chandigarh, when she said, 'It is not easy to convey the true *jazba* (passion or strong emotion) of being a fauji (army man) in simple words.' She meant to say that the intertwined sacrifices and emotional strength of the 'family' of the fauji can only be experienced, not expressed in words. Smiling, she recalled her childhood memory of a jawan reporting to her father, Colonel O.P. Lamba, with the announcement, *'Saab family bhi laya hoon'* (I have brought my family too).

As she peeped from behind her Dadda's (father's) chair, she could see only the jawan's wife standing behind him! Later, Dadda explained to her that for the fauji, his wife is the sum total of 'family', as she represents all ties, related by blood or marriage, sanguine and affinal.

In my debut book, *Kitne Ghazi Aaye, Kitne Ghazi Gaye*, I narrated the real-life story of the mother and children of a soldier of my unit, who died during enemy firing on the LoC, being looked after by the unit, with the commanding officer being the ex-officio guardian of the children. Here I want to narrate another story wherein the paltan ensured that the children of a dead soldier were not only brought up by the unit but also reunited with their mother.

My Unit: My Family

The Shrimad Bhagavad Gita underlines the need and significance of family values and traditions that reinforce a sense of recognition and bonding within the family. These family ties are passed down from generation to generation. Major General Anil Chaudhary, AVSM, narrated the following incident from the days when he was commanding a battalion in the north-eastern region of India:

> I was commanding a battalion in North East in 2002. One day, soon after I took over command of the battalion, I came across a very smart Non-Commissioned Officer (NCO) while playing a cricket match within the unit, and I started engaging with him in a conversation after the match. His fascinating story reiterated how a Unit is truly a family. Many years ago, when this NCO was a young boy, his father was serving as an NCO in the same unit and had turned an alcoholic. Fed up with his ways, his wife left him and shifted permanently to Nepal.

His father died soon after, leaving behind two young boys. The Unit adopted the boys, taking care of their education and upbringing. The bright boys completed their graduation, following which the Unit helped them in getting enrolled as clerks in the Assam Rifles.

I took special interest and got them registered as Personal Assistants (PAs). As the Commanding Officer of the Unit, I now decided to get them settled in life, and discussed the matter with some of the senior JCOs (Junior Commissioned Officers), who had been part of the Unit since the time the boys' father was alive. On my request, one JCO agreed to marry both his daughters, who were of compatible age, with these boys. Once their marriage dates were fixed, both the boys walked into my office, requesting for two months leave, before getting married. It was a rather surprising request as most men would have preferred to avail of their leave after the marriage. When I probed further, the boys said that they wanted to trace their mother before getting married. So, both the brothers were granted leave and as luck would have it, they did manage to trace their mother in Nepal, who had got re-married and had a daughter from the second marriage, though unfortunately she had lost her second husband too. The boys brought their mother and stepsister to the Unit, insisting that the two women participate in their marriage with all fanfare and honour. This tale clearly shows how an Army Unit is truly a family, signifying a home away from home for the Army men.

The Indian Army Breaks Protocol

A soldier may appear to be very strong with his broad shoulders, at times with a big moustache and a heavy voice, but deep inside, he is mostly an emotional and

sensitive person. Soldiers who stay away from their families, especially during field postings, are known to deal with civilians in and around their locations in an extremely friendly manner. Once as the corps commander of Chinar Corps in Kashmir, an unidentified dead body of a seven-year-old boy was recovered from a *nala* named Nala Burzil near village Achhura, on 9 July 2019. This nala flowed from Pakistan-occupied Kashmir (PoK) into the Kishenganga River in the Gurez sector of Kashmir. The infantry battalion responsible for that area immediately swung into action to identify the body. They adopted some non-traditional methods such as using social media in addition to garnering the support of the civil administration; and the deceased was soon identified as Master Abid Ahmed Sheikh, resident of a village near Minimarg in PoK, who had accidently slipped into the nala burzil.

Throughout the day, social media from both sides of the LoC kept buzzing with humanitarian requests and suggestions to hand over the dead body of young Abid. After its identification, contact was established with the Pakistan Army on the hotline, expressing the Indian Army's intent of handing over the body to the family of the deceased. In the absence of a proper mortuary in the remote area and delayed response from the Pakistan Army, the local civil administration offered to conduct the last rites as per the procedures laid down but was persuaded by the army unit to delay the rites. The head maulvi saab and village elders were also taken into confidence to support the noble cause of handing over the dead body to the boy's family. Some locations on the LoC are agreed mutually crossing points but Gurez is not one of them. The nearest crossing point, in Tangdhar sector, was approximately 200 kilometres away and it would have taken a good part of the whole day to travel there by road. The battalion commander thus approached me through his headquarters with a request on humanitarian grounds to hand over the body at a local non-recognized crossing point within the Gurez sector itself, instead of having to transport the body all the way to Tangdhar. This would also make things easier for the boy's parents, preventing the need for them to travel all the way to the Tangdhar crossing point. Meantime, the body had started showing signs of decomposition. We immediately took the decision to hand over the body to the Pakistan Army locally in contravention of the prevailing protocol.

The battalion created a safe lane (removing the mines from the designated area) through the decades-old minefield up to the LoC to ensure that the deceased boy reached his home safely. On 10 July 2019, the battalion tried to hand over the body but the Pakistan Army personnel were reluctant to come close to the LoC. Finally, a day later, a team comprising the unit personnel, led by the commanding officer himself, along with some civil administration officials, walked through the minefield, and handed over the dead body to one Major Mohammed Khan of the Pakistan Army near a Pakistan Army post. This gesture and persistent efforts of the battalion were appreciated by one and all from both sides of the LoC. The Indian Army's noble deed, even going against protocol, also garnered widespread appreciation in both international and national print and electronic media, with the headlines in national newspapers and news channels blaring, 'In a humanitarian gesture, Indian Army hands over the body of a seven-year old child from Pakistan Occupied Kashmir.'

India hands over body of 7-year-old PoK boy to Pak

Child was found in a stream in Gurez sector of Bandipora district

MAJID JAHANGIR
TRIBUNE NEWS SERVICE

SRINAGAR, JULY 11

For a change, camaraderie replaced hostilities on the Line of Control (LoC) after the Army handed over the body of a child, which had flown into a river at this side of Jammu and Kashmir, to the Pakistan army as a goodwill gesture.

Seven-year-old Abid Shaikh, a resident of a village in Gilgit-Baltistan in Pakistan-occupied Kashmir (PoK), had reportedly drowned in a river and his body was fished out in the Gurez sector of Bandipora district on July 9. After efforts for three days by the Indian authorities, the body was handed to Pakistan on Thursday in Gurez.

"In this particular case, instead of returning the mortal remains at the official exchange places like Teetwal, we returned it in the same area so that the mortal remains do not get decomposed. It was a humanitarian gesture," General Officer Commanding of Srinagar-based Chinar Corps, Lt Gen

The body being handed over to the Pakistan army on Thursday.

66 In this particular case, instead of returning the mortal remains at the official exchange place like Teetwal, we returned it in the same area so that the remains do not get decomposed. It was a humanitarian gesture. The body was handed over with full respect and religious rites. 99

 Lt Gen KJS Dhillon, GOC, CHINAR CORPS

KJS Dhillon, said. "The body was handed over with full respect and religious rites. A maulvi ji (religious preacher) was there," he added.

The body of the child was seen by two women in Burzil Nar, a fast-flowing stream that culminates in the Kishanganga river. The Army and civil authorities immediately retrieved the body and made efforts to identify it.

"As no villager from this side claimed the body, a contact was established on the other side of the LoC. The PoK side informed the Army that a boy has been missing from the area of Kamri in Gilgit-Baltistan," an Army officer said. The Army again contacted the Pakistani army and asked it to take back the body.

On Thursday, a physical contact was established along the LoC between the two armies in the Gurez sector for the first time. The LoC in the Gurez sector has remained a constant battlefield over the past nearly three decades as it is one of the key infiltration routes for the militants.

After the PoK boy went missing, his family had also made an appeal through the social media and urged the authorities on both sides to help trace their son.

Boy's body floats to India from PoK, borders melt as soldiers, officials cross minefield for handover

ADIL AKHZER
SRINAGAR, JULY 11

THE BODY of a seven-year-old boy floats down a river from Pakistan to a village in India. There, it is preserved with ice blocks carved out from the mountainside. Finally, an Indian team carries the dead child through a minefield maze to the Line of Control (LoC).

Over the last three days, past many twists and turns, a rare story of heart and heartbreak played out in Achoora village in Gurez valley along the LoC in North Kashmir. On Thursday, the body of Aabid Sheikh was handed over to the Pakistan Army.

"I am seeing such an exchange for the first time in my life," said Nazir Ahmad Gurezi, a former MLA from Gurez, where the body was handed over. **CONTINUED ON PAGE 2**

An Indian team hands over the body of 7-year-old Aabid Sheikh to the Pakistan Army at the LoC in Gurez sector. *Express*

Family Beyond Blood Ties

Here, I wish to narrate another incident wherein a hardworking Kashmiri girl expressed her faith in a senior military commander, asserting that he could help turn her dreams into reality. The girl in question, Ishrat Akther, a twenty-six-year-old wheelchair-bound international basketball and handball player from Jammu and Kashmir, belongs to village Bangdara on the outskirts of Baramulla in North Kashmir. Ishrat is an international medal winner and a motivational speaker who secured first position in the wheelchair race, while competing with ten boys.

In August 2016, when she was only seventeen years old, she had met with an accident wherein she fell from her balcony, which left her with a disability below the waist for the rest of her life. But this did not diminish her never-say-die spirit and the hunger to do something exceptional in life. I have not met Ishrat till date but seeing her social media posts and learning about her performance on the field, I feel as if I have known her for ages. She used to follow me on Instagram and at times I would post motivating comments like 'Well done, Champ,' whenever she posted about her achievements. She would invariably respond to my comments with a routine 'Thank you, Sir'.

On 11 August 2024, more than four and a half years after I had been posted out of Kashmir, and more than two and a half years after I retired from the army, I received a direct message (DM) in my Instagram account box from Ishrat late in the evening. She informed that she had been selected to represent India in the upcoming Third Four-a-Side World Wheelchair Handball World Championship to be held in Cairo, Egypt, in September 2024. She was one of the top ten players selected to represent India on the international stage. She told me that she was not able to book her tickets. I immediately called up

Sabita Chanda, who is part of an initiative called *India Cares*, with whom I had worked during the COVID pandemic in 2021. *India Cares* is not a registered NGO or organization. It is a non-profit, 100 per cent volunteer-run virtual initiative by individuals who dedicate their free time to helping those in need. One of its key initiatives is the Promise Bank, where people register their promises to help; whether by offering financial aid, resources or other forms of support. This initiative connects those in need with those willing to help. Sabita reached out to one of the Promise Bank depositors, who immediately agreed to support Ishrat. The very next day, the depositor booked round-trip flight tickets for Ishrat.

I shared Ishrat's number with Sabita and sent the following message to Ishrat at night itself, 'Dear Ishrat beta, Good evening, Ms Sabita Chanda from India Cares will speak to you. It will be done. You prepare for the camp, Champ (thumbs up emoji).'

To this, Ishrat replied, 'Sir, *yeh beta sun ke* (Sir, listening to this expression of *beta*, meaning 'child'), I can't express how I feel.'

I also received confirmation from Ishrat the next day, 'Tickets done (smiley emoji) all thanks to you and Sabita ma'am. Thank you so much sir.'

I replied, 'Thank you, beta. Now put in your best (thumbs up emoji).'

Looking back on this incident, I feel that my success in helping an aspiring sportsperson who was willing to fight all odds to bring glory to the nation was not so important. What was more important was that she thought of me even after my retirement and believed that a tough military commander like me could be of help for a humane cause in a conflict

zone where alternate narratives rule the roost. It was this very faith in the military commander, expressed by the mothers of young Kashmiri boys who had picked up guns and joined terrorist ranks that led to the success of 'Operation Maa' in the Kashmir Valley, eventually helping to save many young lives. Usually, stories of bloodshed, killings, terrorist atrocities and actions of security personnel make the headlines in a combat zone. However, such humane and peace initiatives in the same zone can make wonderful compassionate and emotional stories that people would love to read. Unfortunately, truth is a long-distance marathoner whereas lies are sprinters.

Military Wives: Strongest Women on the Planet

Today's daughter is tomorrow's mother and a well-brought-up daughter will make a great mother. Napoleon Bonaparte had famously said, 'Give me good mothers and I will give you a good nation! . . . Give me an educated mother, I shall promise you the birth of a civilized, educated nation.'

While answering questions about spouse employment at the 2012 Spouse Summit, Deanie Dempsey, wife of US General Martin E. Dempsey, the chairman of the Joint Chiefs of Staff, once said, 'We as military spouses don't want special treatment, we want fair treatment.'

I firmly believe that military wives are the strongest women on this planet. They not only bring up the children all by themselves while the soldier is performing his duty at the frontline but also look after ageing parents, both their own and those of their husbands, at the same time sacrificing their personal desires to ensure that their husbands are not disturbed while fighting terrorists or the enemy. The quote, 'To become something, you have to sacrifice a whole bunch of everythings' is so apt for military wives.

While military operations and soldiers are always highly commended and appreciated by the government, people and the media, we usually forget to acknowledge the silent contribution made by their families (spouses, parents and children), who keep the home front going against all odds. Having come under terrorist fire myself a number of times, I can admit that ensuring one's own safety is the last thought in a soldier's mind during such situations; but the soldier definitely remembers his family in a 'what if' scenario. In this context, the confidence that their families will be looked after, even after they are gone, is the most motivating factor that pushes soldiers to go beyond all limits in protecting the nation. While in an active firefight, **'I am here and covering you sir, you go for it'**, is the best communication a soldier would ever hear; the family's unspoken support raises similar positive feelings. Simultaneously, we must salute the strong will and forbearance of the families of soldiers and *veer naris* (war widows) in bravely facing all challenges, even without wearing the military boots that their husbands do. The country, society and civil administration owe them a great deal for their silent contribution to the cause of national security. For a corporate employee too, strong family is the kernel for their professional success. Strong family bonds allow each member to cope with their challenges, fully assured of the unwavering support, and maintaining a sense of balance and steadiness.

> '*A family is a place where minds come in contact. If these minds love one another, the home will be as beautiful as a flower garden. But if these minds get out of harmony with one another, it is like a storm that plays havoc with the garden.*'
>
> —Buddha

10

Embracing Success, Fears, Aggression, Regrets and Failures

क्रोधो हर्षश्च दर्पश्च ह्रीस्तम्भो मान्यमानिता ।
यमर्थान्नापकर्षन्ति स वै राजर्षिः उच्यते ॥

*'That person who overwhelms his anger, joy, sorrow and
pride, who has no false modesty, neither confusion nor
vanity, who can stay equanimous in mind at all times, is
undoubtedly in a wise deserving position for leadership.'*

Success—Whys, Hows and Ifs

The dictionary meaning of 'success' is the accomplishment
of an aim or purpose. This definition acquires a deeper
nuance in the military where success is perceived not only as
achieving victory in a campaign or an operation but attaining
this victory with no or minimum casualties to one's own
troops. Thus, a successful military campaign needs to be
clinical and comprehensive as there are no runners-up in
war. This mandate for closing out a military operation with
lethal domination and swift retaliation demands the utmost
level of responsibility (zimmedari) coupled with the highest
obligation of ensuring the safety and well-being of his troops
in the process of winning at all cost.

One of the biggest challenges of a military operation or situation is that no two of them are the same, implying that the leader has to make the winning moves without being able to lean on a precedent or a past experience. It is this challenge that underscores the criticality of on-the-job training, which arms the leader with the ability to handle any unexpected situation with courage and conviction.

The readers may wonder why I am linking 'military training' with 'success'. The answer lies in the fact that in the military, the initial structured training imparted for a specific duration at a pre-commission training academy lays down the blueprint for a soldier's professional future, but unlike other high-profile government professions, this army training is only a teaser. The actual learning comes from persistent on-the-ground experiences that hone each soldier into a lean, mean war machine prepared for any eventuality at short notice. Therefore, each successful operation in the army carries within it the seed of hard work, surgical precision and rigorous training that continue throughout a soldier's working (or more precisely, 'fighting') life.

One of the most significant leadership lessons I have learnt about a leader's behaviour in my long and chequered career, as both one who leads and one who is led by another, lies in this idiom: '**Greet victory like a gentleman and defeat like a man**.' Success thus never comes unbidden but is the outcome of a cumulative effort fostered by hard work, commitment, patience, discipline, passion, perseverance, integrity and, above all, conducive work ethics stemming from regimentation, consistency and confidence.

A recent interaction I had with Jas K. Shan, a renowned life and wellness coach from Chandigarh, re-emphasized

this lesson on handling success for me. Ms Shan told me, 'Sir, you **must always seriously accept compliments** that come your way as you are complimented by only 10 per cent of the people for only 10 per cent of your work; because 90 per cent of the time, people will never compliment you, for they are either jealous of you or feel intimidated by your persona, or simply lack the grace needed to deliver an honest compliment.'

This reminds me of a highly emotional incident that occurred in 2019 in Gulmarg after the abrogation of Article 370 and 35A, when I was the corps commander in Kashmir. A group of Gujarati tourists, who had recognized me among all the officers who were on duty with me, approached my security personnel requesting for a selfie with me. As per protocol, my security team declined their request. However, I approached my security personnel, asking them to allow the tourists to get clicked with me. Soon after the photographs were done, my security staff restored the cordon. Just then, an elderly lady, who must have been around eighty years of age rushed towards me, penetrating the security cordon. Before I realized what was happening, she bent down in an effort to touch my feet in obeisance. I restrained her before she could actually do so. As I encircled her feeble body to lift her from her arched position, she hugged me and said, 'I wish every mother had a son like you.' Deeply humbled at this heartfelt praise, I accepted the compliment wholeheartedly, knowing that it was the best endorsement I had received in my entire life. That woman's gesture was actually a moment of real 'success' for me, as it signified an appreciation of all that my team and I had achieved through hard work as soldiers.

Apart from being the outcome of diligence and persistence, success also has an opportunistic element attached to it. Recall John F. Kennedy's telling quote delivered after the Bay of Pigs fiasco, 'Success has many fathers, but failure is an orphan.' Success also abandons those who are either too afraid to take risks or foolhardy enough to take uncalculated risks without the ability to absorb the fallout. On the other hand, the probability of successes missed when someone doesn't even attempt to do something is a lesson in itself. Another aspect of success is to be confident without being complacent of one's abilities to attain one's goals. It is fraught with danger to be satisfied with the efforts just because it finally came out right; one should only be happy when sure of not getting it wrong ever. Paradoxically, though we are discussing success here, I must caution the reader that the calibre of achievers is measured not by the extent of their success but by the self-confidence with which they handle failure. This was very aptly expressed by the popular singer, late Christina Grimmie, as follows: 'Confidence is not that "they will like me"; confidence instead is "I'll be fine if they don't".' The same sentiment was voiced differently by the indomitable former British prime minister Sir Winston Churchill in these words: 'Success is not final; failure is not fatal: it is the courage to continue that counts.' **A decorated soldier will always have a pair of rough hands, a soft heart and bruised shoulders.**

Fear Prompting Aggression

Fear is defined in the dictionary as an unpleasant human emotion that is usually caused by the anticipation or awareness of danger. As discussed in an earlier chapter, fear is just ignorance tackled by intelligent and persistent action. Fear or apprehension can cause aggression, which is akin to a natural defence mechanism or a primal survival response that acts as a shield against the feeling of being threatened or overwhelmed. It is well known that negative emotions such as fear, anger, pain and frustration can lead to aggression, especially when accompanied by a feeling of excitability. In leadership parlance, an aggressive mindset also has some positive intonations, as it is viewed as a retaliatory action to be unleashed at the right moment against an enemy or competitor but never against one's own countrymen or own team. It is important to clarify here that the term 'aggression' does not signify violence or abusiveness, but an aggressive mindset is, at times, required for taking bold decisions and motivating the team members to deliver even beyond their capacity. Till the moment to unleash the aggression arrives, a leader must be the most humble person.

The biggest apprehension of a military leader is not one of suffering personal physical injuries in an operation but that of losing men in enemy or terrorist fire. This fear of the loss of a colleague or team member constantly nettles a soldier's mind, concealing their fears and emotions beneath a tough exterior symbolized by their impressive physique or fighting prowess. Fear is a genuine human behaviour under threat and hence every soldier or commander is equally prone to it. When under threat, a young soldier will take longer to regain composure as compared to an experienced one. This again underscores the importance of on-the-job training and real battle experience. In the absence of actual battlefield experience, the soldiers are made to undergo 'battle inoculation', which simulates a battlefield scenario, replete with the actual firing of weapons such as artillery guns, mortars, medium machine guns and rocket launchers.

Taking a cue from this, corporate houses would do well to train their employees in handling the visualized critical situations during simulated workshop sessions.

Fear has, in fact, been characterized as a crucial response to danger, enabling humans to summon courage in the face of the most daunting situation. On the other hand, the absence of fear would prevent human beings from training themselves to handle any kind of threat, physical or psychological. Though it may seem a bit paradoxical, in extreme circumstances, fear can actually act as a motivation to perform beyond one's own physical and psychological limits. I am reminded of a story I heard a few years ago. A young man walking past a graveyard at night suddenly slipped and fell into a freshly dug grave. All his attempts to pull himself out of the grave proved futile. Frustrated and defeated, he lay in one corner of the grave when a middle-aged man walking on the road above met with the same fate and fell into the same grave beside him. He also tried his best to come out of the grave but was unsuccessful. Realizing that the middle-aged man could not see him in the dark, the young man decided to play a prank and started emitting ghostly sounds. Mortified by the eerie noise, the middle-aged man desperately tried to climb out of the grave. Although he failed repeatedly, the rising fear ultimately instilled in him an almost superhuman strength, and he was able to get a grip on the upper surface and pull himself out of the grave. This story demonstrates how extreme fear can act as a great motivating factor, enabling one to perform ostensibly impossible feats.

In the battlefield too, it is often fear that imparts mental toughness to a soldier. Coupled with complete faith in his weapon, buddy and commander, this apprehension is

converted into bravado for the soldier, allowing him to take on the enemy with renewed courage. And in a simulated training ground, a military leader sets easy and achievable targets for the young soldiers, teaching them to identify, negotiate with and eventually overcome all their fears.

Regrets and Feelings of Guilt

Recently, when I was delivering a motivational talk at a prestigious school at Pathankot, a girl student asked me the following question during an interaction with the audience, 'Sir, when a soldier kills a terrorist, does he ever feel any guilt or regret at killing another human who is also someone's son?' Although I was shaken by this question from a young student, I responded calmly in a very measured manner so as to not disturb a young mind. I quoted from the Shrimad Bhagavad Gita, citing the incident when a dismayed Arjuna refused to fight his near and dear ones in the Kaurava army, who, however, were ready to indulge in a war with their close friends and relatives. The inspiring words uttered by Shri Krishna, exhorting Arjuna to go ahead and fight the Kauravas and perform his dharma (righteous duty) as a warrior, signify the true spirit of a soldier's life and his commitment to defend the honour of his army, regardless of who the foe on the other side of the battleground may be. This diligence towards his duty also eliminates any feeling of regret or guilt in a soldier, who is literally out to fulfil his 'day's work' without getting trapped by any distractions! Hence, while carrying out one's righteous duty in good faith, there is no scope of having a feeling of guilt or regret. The fact that only a few fortunate ones among us do not harbour feelings of guilt, regret or unfounded fears is evocatively expressed in the story 'The Judo Kid'.

A ten-year-old boy decided to study judo despite the fact that he had lost his left arm in a devastating car accident. The boy began lessons with an old Japanese judo master. The boy was doing well, so he couldn't understand why, after three months of training, the master had taught him only one move.

'Sensei,' the boy finally said, 'shouldn't I be learning more moves?'

'This is the only move you know, but it is the only move you'll ever need to know,' the sensei replied.

Not quite understanding, but believing in his teacher, the boy kept training. Several months later, the sensei took the boy to his first tournament.

Surprising himself, the boy easily won his first two matches. The third match was more difficult, but his opponent soon became impatient and charged; the boy deftly used his only move to win the match.

Still amazed by his success, the boy was now in the finals. This time, his opponent was bigger and stronger. Concerned that the boy might get hurt, the referee called a time-out.

He was about to stop the match when the sensei intervened. 'No,' the sensei insisted, 'let him continue.'

Soon after the match resumed, his opponent made a critical mistake: he dropped his guard. Instantly, the boy used his move to pin him.

The boy won the match and the tournament.

'Sensei, how did I win with only one move?'

'You won for two reasons,' the sensei answered. 'First, you've mastered one of the most difficult throws in all of judo. And second, the only defence for that move is for your opponent to grab your left arm.'

The boy's biggest weakness had become his biggest strength.

Sometimes we feel that we have certain weaknesses and we blame the circumstances and ourselves for it but we never know that our weakness can become our strength one day.[8]

I have imbibed two lessons from this tale. First, always believe in your teacher; and second, every situation has a positive side and invariably, it's the other side. The spark of sunlight can penetrate even a tough wall if it finds only a minuscule crack in it, so being slightly imperfect will allow the light to come into a dark room. Conrad Hall, the renowned cinematographer, is remembered for his quote, 'There's a kind of beauty in imperfection.' I often quote this famous couplet by the renowned Indian poet Firaq Gorakhpuri before those who feel they have missed something in life: '*Paal le ek rog nadaan zindagi ke vaste, sirf sehat ke sahare umar toh katati nahi* (Innocent one, adopt an affliction for the sake of life, life cannot be lived with only good health).'

Failures

It all begins in the mind: As they say, both positivity and negativity originate in the mind, shaping our thoughts, actions and personalities throughout our lives. Our thoughts sculpt who we are and who we will become. The human mind is one of the most complex repositories of our conscious and subconscious entities, determining our sensory and physical perceptions, and enabling us to think, feel, perceive, imagine and remember. It also conditions

---

[8] Source : https://www.dailytenminutes.com/2016/01/story-judo-kid.html?m=1

our behaviour and response to various situations and experiences.

One of the most critical emotions that take birth in the human mind is fear, especially the fear of failure, which can act as a huge mental block, impeding all our actions, and actually preventing us from succeeding in all our endeavours. This is fittingly articulated by the popular Indian actor Anupam Kher, when he says, 'The pain of failure is less than the pain of regret of not attempting it . . . Go for it.' Failures are not only an integral part of life but also the most fundamental teacher about life. During my career, I always refrained from judging any individual based on the results of their actions, rather than the diligence and commitment behind those actions.

In the army, the real test of an individual's commitment lies in the manner in which they face the enemy. The same person may be able to produce the desired results in peacetime activities like sports, or training or administrative tasks due to favourable environmental factors but may fail to replicate the same success in the battlefield where they come face to face with a ruthless opponent, who will leave no stone unturned to ensure one's failure. Anupam Kher hits the nail on the head when he defines failure as 'an event, never a person'.

Interestingly, the track record of many people who have attained remarkable success in their lives and respective professions reveals that they failed a lot more than they succeeded. Harsha Bhogle, cricket commentator, quotes the highly successful former cricketer and captain of the Indian team, Rahul Dravid, who believes that failure is an integral part of life, as in cricket too. Dravid batted 604 times for India

but failed to reach fifty runs in as many as 410 of those innings, thus recording more failures than successes in his cricketing career. Thus, like cricket, in life too, failure often lays the foundation for future success, offering the opportunity for a better outcome in the 'second innings'. In one of his most poignant speeches, former US President Barack Obama told a group of schoolchildren, 'The first book by the author of the Harry Potter series, J.K. Rowling, was rejected twelve times before finally being accepted for publication. Michael Jordan, the inimitable basketball legend, was removed from his high school's basketball team and lost hundreds of games and missed thousands of shots during his career. His comment was, "I have failed over and over and over again in my life. And that is why I succeed."' Obama's words signify the most potent teaching for children—to accept defeat over and over again without giving up the effort to win the next time, as there will be a next time!

Resilience is the most profound human ability to adapt and recover from difficult life situations and bounce back from adversity. Those who nurture this trait can also better handle stress, failure and even more importantly, the apprehension of failing. A leader's calibre is thus tested less by how successful he is, and more by how he handles or celebrates failure as a stepping stone to success. We all have read the story of King Robert the Bruce of Scotland, who was inspired by a resilient spider to fight the English and regain his kingdom. A dynamic leader must also always keep evolving and never allow inertia in his actions or thoughts. Leadership is learning the art to celebrate a failure by viewing it as a chance to adapt and discover contemporary propositions.

Never Reinforce a Failure is one of the most important lessons of warfare. A soldier is trained to accept temporary setbacks, and the need to modify plans mid-course if things do not go as anticipated. This concept of never reinforcing a failure is reiterated in the Japanese saying, 'If you get on the wrong train, immediately get off at the nearest station, for the longer it takes you to get off, the more expensive will the return trip be.' So folks, remember, '**It's not over when you lose, it's over only when you quit.**' My poetic take on failure is:

> *'Tootna buri baat nahi, toot ke bikharna bhi*
> *buri baat nahi;*
> *Toot ke judna himmat hai, aur judke udna*
> *himmat hai'*

(There is nothing wrong in falling apart, what is unacceptable is to allow yourself to disintegrate if you fall apart. Summon the courage to get back after a setback, and rise like a phoenix from the ashes of failure.)

'*Life loses half its interest if there is no struggle—if there are no risks to be taken.*'

—Netaji Subhas Chandra Bose

11

I Recognize the Brilliance Within You

नाप्राप्यमभिवाञ्छन्ति नष्टं नेच्छन्ति शोचितुम्
आपत्सु च न मुह्यन्ति नराः राजर्षिः बुद्धयः

'*They who do not strive for things with detrimental consequences, who do not grieve for what is lost, who do not suffer in their minds even while facing severe calamities, are to be regarded as intellectuals who have realized the wisdom in their life. Only such a person makes the most exceptional leader.*'

I began writing this book after a brief interaction with a lady in February 2024, who told me, 'I see what shines in you.' Her exceptional and totally unexpected words of acclaim took me completely by surprise, but they also set me thinking as to what character traits can make an individual 'shine', and how deep does this glitter radiate within one's personality? Is it just a superfluous gloss or does it reflect an innate sparkle that spreads light outside?

While writing this book, page by page, word by word, it has gradually become clear to me that the 'shine' on the surface is a window into an inner glow that absorbs light from the people and happenings around me; and has slowly but surely made space for '**recognizing the brilliance within**'.

Here I would like to clarify that this brilliance is not mine alone but emanates equally within every officer and soldier of the defence forces that I have had the privilege to work with. It gets rubbed on to a soldier consciously and at times subconsciously as they navigate through various stages of their lives, from a raw young boy to an officer and I daresay 'a gentleman'.

As I understand, this process involves the chiselling of a military leader, imbibing of the military leadership ethos and traditions, learning the ropes of regimentation and the honour codes of the army, building teams, owning your organization, balancing emotions with hardcore duties, respecting family values, navigating crises, facing up to challenges, sustaining passion and motivation, making tough choices and, above all, not allowing yourself to be broken by withstanding the unbearable pressure for that crucial one second more. While describing these different phases of a soldier's life, this book showcases how each of them contributes to the making of a true leader, imparting the qualities and ethics that dominate military war rooms and that can be used with equal flair to achieve success in corporate boardrooms.

On the issue of 'shine', I must say that spectators may eye your trophies and awards with envy but they may be oblivious to the sweat and the grime that goes into earning them. At times, even those expressing appreciation for others' awards suggest that winning them has been a stroke of good luck for them. It is to these and such other people that I wish to clarify that attributing this recognition to mere good fortune undermines the success and effort that

go into earning accolades. Good luck and hard work go hand in hand. As the saying goes, a hardworking person may be lucky, but no one can be lucky unless they are hardworking. As a soldier and now an author, I believe that this hard work is bound to make the next chapter of my life awesome and awe-inspiring for the next generations. In the army, we believe that history may be shaped by destiny but destiny is shaped through the diligence, discipline and daring of the soldier. Once during a recital, a famous singer said that acceptance is power, suggesting that divine actions are beyond human understanding and we must learn to accept things beyond our control as the 'Will of God'. However, willpower is a strange foible that can challenge the quirks of fate, as exemplified by a few great men who have carved history by defying destiny.

Our thoughts and actions often oscillate between the extremes of emotions and sensibilities, but we should remember that life thrives only in equilibrium. And this equilibrium can be achieved only by balancing extremes, by nurturing all aspects of life, including work, personal development, relationships, health and spirituality. Similarly, a leader, too, needs to find balance and harmony between their mission, team, expectations and the objective to be achieved. Leadership is synonymous with inclusivity, as a leader needs to respect diverse and divergent perspectives and individuals, ensuring that each member of the team feels empowered and valued, leading to better results and a positive work environment.

In the Indian context, spirituality (distinct from religion) is an important attribute that imparts meaning and purpose to one's mission, fostering well-being, strength of character and a calmer disposition in an otherwise chaotic universe. Indian culture, imbued with ancient wisdom spanning over 5000 years of civilization, is a rich blend of heritage, faiths and traditions. As custodians of this culture and its offshoots, we need to take pride in our ancestry and maintain our cultural values and traditions while seamlessly adapting to modern ways of life, especially advancements in technology. Similarly, in the army, every soldier is trained to follow the traditions and honour codes without compromising on accomplishment of the mission at hand.

'Don't try to become the jewellery. Just aim to become pure gold in the first place and the process will gradually turn you into jewellery.' This was my curt advice to a Class XI student aspiring to join the defence forces when he asked me on Instagram how he could become a Special Forces officer. I further advised him to study diligently and prepare meticulously for the Services Selection Board (SSB) after clearing the UPSC written examination. After selection in the SSB, having cleared the medical tests and finding a place in the merit list, he would have to undergo four years of pre-commission training. Finally, he could opt for commissioning in a regiment of his choice on successful completion of the training. Just as every process in nature takes its own time, success also comes in good time. Without attempting to circumvent any of the processes, one should supplement them with hard work, commitment and innovativeness.

I conclude this book with a few words of counsel for young and impressionable minds based on my experiences of leading teams over nearly four decades.

- Success doesn't have the option of 'free home delivery'.
- Your life, you decide; but expert advice helps.
- Focus on efforts and processes, the results will happen automatically.
- Treat failures like lessons and use them as occasions for planning better to achieve success the next time.
- Dare to Aim. Set aims. War-game your options before taking a leap.
- Plan your strategies and options but go along with the situations as they unfold.
- Life is never going to be an easy game. Play hard.
- Never hesitate to venture into new ideas, but maintain sharp focus on achieving your aims. Small start-up initiatives only go on to become unicorns.
- Maintain your unique character and individuality, but be flexible enough to blend with your team without compromising on your core values.
- Competence and hard work will inevitably bring success, but success also leads to jealousy and ill-will. Stay away from such negative people. Remember the saying: 'You can't change the people around you but you can change the people around you.'
- Those who are in a position to help also retain the ability to hurt. So, always keep your guard up.
- There will be times when it is absolutely fine to seek help. Asking for help isn't giving up; it's refusing to give up.
- Hard work needs regular practice.
- Pamper and indulge yourself once in a while, as you are the most important person in your life. Even airline crews tell you 'first wear your own face mask

before helping others'. All work and no play makes Jack a dull boy.

- Life gives everyone at least one chance to attain greatness. Grab that chance. Take bold decisions in the face of adversity.
- Never be afraid of people's opinions. History in any case will judge.
- Respect heroes. Always remember the Unknown Soldier who laid down their life in the line of duty unacknowledged. Not every hero finds a mention in the honour roll.
- Human efficiency does improve with age; though paradoxically, leaders may also become more rigid and less flexible to change as they grow older.
- Delegation is not dilution of authority, it is dispersal of decision-making at different levels, allowing more time for strategic thinking at higher levels.
- At the end of the day, you may not be half as bad as people will make you out to be. So, bash on regardless.
- Subtle humour can liven up any war room or boardroom, chiefly when it comes from the leader.
- When it is an un-defendable straight punch, take it on the chin.
- Work for your organization as if you own that organization.
- A soldier desires peace but remains prepared for war; count your blessings but never forget to pray.
- Nation First Always. For a soldier, the tricolour is not just a flag, but a symbol of sacrifice, courage and unwavering duty towards the nation. A soldier of the

Indian Army follows only one religion—service to the motherland.

- **'Awe Factor':** A leader must recognize and celebrate other people's success. This entails following a simple 'A' model:
  - □ **Accept**, even by a small nod of the head, that the work of your team members or others has been noticed.
  - □ **Acknowledge** their efforts and skills.
  - □ **Admire** the positive difference their presence is making to the organization.
  - □ **Appreciate** others for making you a better person, professionally and socially.
  - □ **AWE**. Finally, turn **'A'** (a single individual) into **'WE'** (a collective team).

At the end of the day, yours must be a well-lived life.

किरदार शिद्दत से निभाइये ज़िन्दगी में
कहानी एक दिन सभी को होना है

(Enact your role with passion and intensity while you are around, for ultimately, like everyone else, you too will become a story to be told.)

Jai Hind

Acknowledgements

'**H**um nahi changge, bura nahin koi' (I am not good, no one is bad) is a very meaningful verse from the Sri Guru Granth Sahib Ji, emphasizing humility and recognizing the inherent worth of all fellow humans. I cite these thought-provoking words that express a deep sense of modesty and humility towards all beings, for it is one human personality trait that makes a leader stay grounded all the time, irrespective of the success achieved.

I once again begin the acknowledgements for my book with a bow in reverence and an utmost feeling of pride and gratitude for all the brave-hearts among my colleagues and peers who made the supreme sacrifice in the service of the nation. With prayers on my lips and pride in my heart, I salute them with a swollen chest and a promise that their sacrifices will motivate future generations in the years to come.

My first and foremost thanks, of course, once again go to my wife of more than thirty-eight years, Nita, and our son and daughter, who wholeheartedly supported my honest way of living throughout my service life and even to date. I am also eternally thankful to my family for their understanding and quiet acceptance of the challenges of an army life that allowed me the space to fulfil my duties with *Wafadari, Imaandari* and *Zimmedari*. My family's unflinching support helped me relentlessly perform my duty towards the nation without fear or favour, with utmost professional integrity and diligence, a duty that I would willingly and happily fulfil again if ever the need arises.

Military leadership ethos may have been formally taught to me in the pre-commission academies and subsequently during on-the-job training in the army. But I would like to confess here that my first teacher of human values was Bijee, my maternal grandmother, who groomed me through my early childhood and during my growing-up years.

I was singularly fortunate to be chiselled and moulded during my initial days in the 4th Battalion the Rajputana Rifles by Brigadier Trigunesh Mukherjee, AVSM (Retd), my first commanding officer and a veritable father figure. It may be easy to learn the military ethos as a youngster but what is most difficult is to be able to withstand the tremendous environmental and professional challenges and live by the honour codes as a senior commander. I want to put on record my professional appreciation for my commanders, who allowed me space to work with full operational freedom and follow the ethics of *Wafadari, Imaandari* and *Zimmedari*. Brigadier Shashi Nair, the late Major General Ravi Thodge, Lieutenant General Ranbir Singh and the late General Bipin Rawat were a few such heroes.

I learnt the core values that shaped me into an officer who made a difference from the best of regimental junior commissioned officers and non-commissioned officers in the Rajputana Rifles throughout my career, right from my freshman days, when I joined the army as a second lieutenant. I apologize for not mentioning names here but I acknowledge each and every soldier who has been instrumental in making me what I am today.

The first person outside my professional and personal family I would like to acknowledge is Premanka Goswami, associate publisher at Penguin Random House India, who brainstormed the idea, format, layout and flow of the book with me for more than a year before I put my pen to paper. Once armed with all the necessary ammunition, I was ready with the manuscript in less than six months thereafter. As we say in the army, 'The time spent on the reconnaissance is never wasted'; so also the year-plus spent on the initial discussions produced the end-product, which wouldn't have been the same but for the guidance of a professional editor to a soldier trying to be an author. 'Premanka, we rock as a team; great job, buddy.'

My sincerest thanks go to Anupma Mehta, who shaped the narrative and contributed perceptively in bringing this book to life. Her editorial craft has imparted deep meaning to the expressions in the book, while intuitively capturing my mind vibes and portraying graphic pictures of events that have encapsulated my career and life in the army. She has indeed been a vital motivator in my second avatar as a writer. I can say with confidence and conviction that her valuable inputs have taken us a long way, and both my books have come out better with Anupma's contribution. I acknowledge her talent as an extraordinary editor and look forward to continuing this partnership with her through any possible future endeavours.

In conclusion, I have to mention **Bolt**, our third baby and pet with a royal black coat, who was our most wafadar friend for nearly fourteen years. Unfortunately, Bolt left us in August 2023 after many years of companionship. Stay faithful, buddy, wherever you are. Love you always, Bolt!

Jai Hind.

Scan QR code to access the
Penguin Random House India website